Andrew Mason and Groupon

INTERNET BIOGRAPHIES™

Andrew Mason and
Groupon

PHILIP WOLNY

ROSEN
PUBLISHING®
New York

For Adriana Vladuca

Published in 2013 by The Rosen Publishing Group, Inc.
29 East 21st Street, New York, NY 10010

First Edition

Library of Congress Cataloging-in-Publication Data

Wolny, Philip.
Andrew Mason and Groupon/Philip Wolny.—1st ed.
    p. cm.—(Internet biographies)
Includes bibliographical references and index.
ISBN 978-1-4488-6916-9 (library binding)
1. Mason, Andrew, 1981– 2. Groupon (Firm) 3. Coupons (Retail trade)
4. Internet marketing. 5. Internet advertising. I. Title.
HF6127.W65 2013
381'.142—dc23

2011043086

Manufactured in the United States of America

CPSIA Compliance Information: Batch #S12YA: For further information, contact Rosen Publishing, New York, New York, at 1-800-237-9932.

Contents

INTRODUCTION

Imagine you wanted to go snowboarding or surfing, take karate lessons, or take part in some other cool activity. Let's say a day of snowboarding, with lessons, equipment, and lift tickets, costs about $100. The problem is that you don't have enough cash to pay for it. But you go online and see an offer of a complete snowboarding package for just $20. You are excited... but is it too good to be true?

These days, it probably isn't. One of the most innovative and popular Web sites of the past decade, Groupon.com, is just the place to find such deals. Groupon is a Web-based service that e-mails vouchers to subscribers every day. These vouchers can be used to receive discounted goods and services (usually 50 to 90 percent off the usual price) from participating and popular local businesses. Started in Chicago, Illinois, Groupon has expanded to dozens of cities all around the world.

Perhaps just as interesting as the business practices of Groupon is the story of its founder, Andrew Mason. Only in his early thirties, he leads what is, according to *Forbes*, the fastest-growing company ever. A musician, computer programmer, and entrepreneur, Mason has designed a company as colorful and untraditional as himself.

Groupon founder and CEO Andrew Mason is photographed while taking part in Allen & Company's Media and Technology Conference in Sun Valley, Idaho. This is a week-long conference described as a "summer camp for moguls," where technology leaders discuss issues and make deals.

Mason's billion-dollar idea, which grew out of an earlier Web site, the Point, has revolutionized e-commerce. Along the way, he has amazed observers with how quickly Groupon has grown—it now has more than 35 million registered users in 250 markets around the world. Mason has further contributed to this growth by buying up smaller competing sites that copied the Groupon model.

Groupon's runaway success and popularity has attracted a lot of interest, especially among prospective investors and larger Internet-based companies wishing to buy out Mason's company. Yet Mason showed little inclination to compromise his dreams and sell off his ideas for a quick payout. When Internet giants Yahoo! and Google offered $3 billion and $6 billion, respectively, to buy the company in 2010, Mason and his partners decided to continue on independently—at least for the time being. In the wake of these failed purchase offers, Groupon "went public" in November 2011. Groupon sold ownership shares of its company to investors. Each share—or stock—was initially sold for $20, valuing the company at $12.8 billion. On the first day of trading Groupon shares rose 31 percent from that level, valuing the company at $16.7 billion.

It has not all been smooth sailing for Mason and Groupon. Legal challenges have arisen, and Groupon has had to refine and improve its business model in response to market realities. New "clone" companies are seemingly copying Groupon all around the world. Many larger Internet companies are now offering very similar services, including LivingSocial, Google Offers, and Facebook Deals. But Groupon has taken the good and the bad in stride, using setbacks, challenges, and competition to learn valuable lessons and improve its strategies for continued growth and worldwide expansion.

Along the way, Mason hopes to never lose the exuberant and joyful spirit that has brought him this far. As he wrote in Groupon's initital public offering (IPO), "Life is too short to be a boring company." Known for playful pranks and a lively sense of humor, Mason is nonetheless a serious businessman who has sought out valuable lessons from helpful mentors along the way. He is a workaholic and a serious thinker and innovator, much like his contemporaries Sergey Brin and Larry Page, the founders of Google, and Mark Zuckerberg, creator of Facebook.

While it is too early to tell what will happen in the long term, Groupon seems poised to become one of the greatest online success stories of the twenty-first century. Let's explore the story of Groupon, one of the fastest-growing companies ever.

CHAPTER 1

Before Groupon

Many well-known pioneers and innovators experience success early on. Andrew Mason demonstrated a mind for business since adolescence, though even his early successes could not have predicted the way he would take the Internet by storm before reaching his thirtieth birthday.

EARLY PROMISE

Andrew Mason was born in 1981, the son of Bob Mason and Bridgit Wolf. He grew up just outside of Pittsburgh, Pennsylvania, in an upper-middle-class suburb called Mount Lebanon. Though his family was well-off, Andrew experienced adversity following his parents' separation when he was seven years old. He and his sister mainly lived with their mother, but they spent time with both their parents.

His parents both had their own businesses—his mother was a photographer, and his father was a diamond dealer. As a youngster, Andrew also wanted to earn his

Andrew Mason poses on the grand staircase of the Art Institute of Chicago, one of Groupon's earliest daily deals clients. Part of Mason's business mission is to encourage users to try new experiences, including visiting cultural institutions.

own money. However, it was often the project itself, rather than its potential profit, that was his greatest motivation. "I think I was probably that kid in the neighborhood who you could expect once or twice a year to be knocking on your door trying to sell you something stupid," he told *Vanity Fair* in August 2011.

Andrew showed signs of leadership, charisma, and salesmanship early on. "He was absolutely the leader," his mother told the *Chicago Tribune* in December 2010. "He could talk [his friends] into doing things they had no intention of doing."

Like many entrepreneurs, he did not always see eye-to-eye with authority figures, especially when it came to his moneymaking ideas. Noticing that his friends in high school always seemed to have spare change on them, he saw a business opportunity. He would buy candy in bulk outside of school and then sell it in the school cafeteria—that is, until the school cafeteria workers put a stop to it, as he related to the *Pittsburgh Post-Gazette* in November 2010. But it was an early sign that Andrew, instead of following the status quo, was looking beyond it, even if he had to take risks.

MASON'S FIRST VENTURES

The young Andrew dreamed about working at the toy superstore Toys 'R' Us. However, when he finally landed a job there, he lasted about a week. It seemed that being his own boss was his true path.

At the age of fifteen, Andrew launched another of his early business ventures: Bagel Express. Its business model was similar to that of his aborted candy-selling operation. He would buy bagels in bulk at a 40 percent discount and then deliver them on Saturday mornings to home customers in his area. He charged his neighbors full price, plus a delivery fee.

Other short-lived entrepreneurial ventures included a computer repair business, which he started with another high school friend. His confidence led him to try anything, even if it was beyond his talents or skills at the time. "I was really into computers, but I was way overconfident," he told the *Pittsburgh Post-Gazette*. "We'd go to someone's house, take the lid off, nod, and sometimes fix things, sometimes not." Though some success was mixed with generous amounts of failure in this venture, it was Andrew's characteristic natural curiosity, and a fearless trial-and-error approach, that would serve him well years later.

FINDING A MENTOR

In 1999, he enrolled at Chicago's Northwestern University, entering the engineering program. He had played piano from an early age and played in a rock band from high school into his college years. Eventually, his interest in a possible music career prompted him to become a music major. Chicago is renowned as a musical and artistic town and, at that time, was especially celebrated for its alternative rock scene.

While at Northwestern, Mason secured an internship with musician and producer Steve Albini at Albini's Electrical Audio studios. Albini was known for producing many legendary alternative artists, including Nirvana and the Pixies, and for being hardworking and opinionated. In many ways, he was as legendary in the music scene as were any of the bands he produced records for.

Famed Chicago-based music producer and sound engineer Steve Albini was one of Andrew Mason's early musical mentors. He is shown here performing with his band Shellac at the All Tomorrow's Parties music festival in Minehead, England.

Albini's intern made an impression on him. As Albini later told *Vanity Fair*, some of Mason's ideas seem crazy at first, "[but] he can very quickly abandon a bad idea and pick up a good idea without being interrupted by inertia. He is one of the most nimble thinkers I've ever run into." Mason also showed some of the fun-loving team spirit that he brought to his later efforts. For example, he created T-shirts depicting every one of his fellow Electrical Audio staff.

Albini became one of Mason's mentors, and Mason credits the producer with teaching him valuable lessons about work and craft. "[Albini] had a really strong philosophy about what he did and why he did it," he told the *Pittsburgh Post-Gazette*, referring to Albini's practice of charging relatively low producing fees for projects that he believed in. "He, by his own choice, lives his own humble, modest life." It was Albini's ability to balance the pursuit of wealth with the desire to engage in creative work that would have a positive impact on the world that Mason absorbed and carried forward in his own future pursuits.

While studying music at Northwestern and interning with Albini, Mason also taught himself computer programming, including Web design. However, he graduated from Northwestern in 2003 without any concrete plans for the future. For the time being, he continued working as a programmer. In later years, when writing his official bio for the Groupon Web site, he downplayed his programming skills, writing, "Andrew became a software developer by no ambitions of his own, but via a series of acquaintances offering to give him money to do incrementally harder stuff on computers."

INNERWORKINGS

In January 2006, he was hired by InnerWorkings to be the lead software developer. Brian McCormack and Rich Heis started InnerWorkings in 2001, with the financial support of fellow Internet entrepreneur Eric Lefkofsky. Their company developed software and systems that helped midsized companies order and manage printing services.

Mason befriended Lefkofsky, already an industry veteran who had started numerous Internet-related companies and projects. Lefkofsky soon became Mason's newest mentor. The experienced entrepreneur was as impressed with Mason as Albini had been earlier.

BACK TO SCHOOL: POLICY TREE

In the fall of 2006, Mason left InnerWorkings to go back to school. This time, he attended the University of Chicago's Harris School of Public Policy. He had decided to apply his computer skills to a new discipline—the laws, regulations, courses of action, funding priorities, and decision making that governments initiate for the public good.

Mason's studies led to the creation of Policy Tree (http://www.policytree.org), a Web-based software application that allowed users to track the progress of various policy proposals and initiatives and present their own arguments and debates over public policy. Policy Tree worked by creating graphic organizers to display the various arguments and points of view associated with a compelling issue or debate.

For example, one of the site's final posts, in 2007, featured the following statement to be debated: "The Bush administration broke the law by secretly authorizing wiretaps on U.S. citizens." This statement is placed within a box at the top of the Web page. From this box extend lines connecting to other boxes that continue to branch off each other. Each of these boxes contains a user's response to the central proposition and to other users' responses. Green lines indicate that a box supports the idea above it, while red lines point toward a statement that refutes it. So one response that is connected by a red line to the central proposition states, "These wiretaps are necessary for national security." Another box connected to and beneath it responds, "This isn't being questioned—the only issue here is why the president decided to go around the normal rules that govern such surveillance, why he chose to make himself above the law." The debate flows and branches out from the main proposition as users react both to it and to other users' arguments and counterarguments.

The Web 2.0 Revolution That Made Groupon Possible

The Internet craze of the late 1990s was driven by e-commerce—the shifting of everyday shopping for goods and services away from brick-and-mortar stores toward online Web retailers and service providers. The next great Internet boom period arrived early in the first decade of the twenty-first century with "Web 2.0." This ushered in the era of user-generated content, wikis, blogs, video sharing, mobile apps, and perhaps most importantly, online social networking.

Social media—from earlier examples like Friendster, Classmates.com, and MySpace, to modern phenomena like Facebook—include Internet communities and networks that allow users to connect for dating, the sharing of common interests, and the exchanging of information and other media. With an Internet connection, which became increasingly available through Wi-Fi, people from the next street over or half a world away could come together to communicate and share information of all kinds. The growing popularity of mobile, Internet-enabled devices like iPhones and Blackberrys seemed to make social media an unstoppable growth market and a wide-open frontier of opportunity.

In effect, Policy Tree facilitated political discussion and the airing out of issues while revealing the wide range of public opinions. It also provided a graphic illustration of how such discussion flows and branches and splits off into secondary issues that may or may not be related to the central matter at hand.

Mason believed that Policy Tree was a great way for people to learn about a new issue—and maybe even challenge their own beliefs. At the very least, working on the site allowed him to further develop his programming, coding, and Web site development skills. These would serve him well in the near future and on the long road to success ahead.

THE "TIPPING POINT": ONLINE SOCIAL ACTIVISM

Mason's next venture, the Point, was named after one of the ideas that interested him at the time. The idea was the so-called "tipping point," following which certain events are set into irrevocable motion. Writer Malcolm Gladwell popularized the concept in his influential book, also titled *The Tipping Point*, published in 2000. Gladwell believed that a certain number had to be reached in any system before a momentous, lasting, or irreversible change occurred.

Mason designed the Point to be a tool for people wishing to engage in group action for the betterment of society. He hoped it would primarily encourage people to pursue social change. For example, suppose someone was circulating an online petition demanding that Congress strike down a certain unfair law. The activists could set up their petition within the Point. The petition would not be activated and sent to Congress until it received at least five thousand signatures. In this case, five thousand signatures would be the tipping point. That number would represent a sufficient groundswell of public opinion to justify sending the petition on to congressional decision makers. Mason would create a platform that would let people band together with others to achieve a particular goal, express a collective opinion, or launch a mass protest.

The Point was very much a creation that fit its era. The new site was part of a wave of Internet-based platforms in the 2000s that took advantage of people's hunger for social networking and virtual community building. The Internet had long been a place where people could gather to explore common interests: gaming, literature, superhero movies, gardening, cooking, and literally millions of other pursuits. Why not create something that would let people mobilize, whether to change the world, pressure political and business leaders, have a say in public and corporate policy, or simply get a better deal on goods and services? In this way, the seeds were sown for the idea that would later become Groupon.

A CASH INFUSION

Eric Lefkofsky, Mason's mentor, was impressed with the concepts behind, and the enormous potential of, the Point. "There was almost nothing like it on the Web," he told *Vanity Fair*. Lefkofsky agreed to fund this new project of Mason's. This financial support was based on Mason's earlier work on Policy Tree and on the strength of the new idea.

Andrew Mason is pictured here leaving a conference meeting held at the Sun Valley Inn during the Sun Valley Media and Technology Conference. He is walking with one of his mentors, Groupon investor and entrepreneur Eric Lefkofsky.

In a typically humble fashion, Mason downplayed his own role in getting the Point up and running. Lefkofsky approached Mason, who was still pursuing his public policy studies at the University of Chicago, after hearing about his idea for the new site. He summoned him to his office and, as Mason told Mixergy.com in July 2010, told him, "'Here's how it works. You can keep going to school or you can work on this idea. We'll fund it, and you can be entrepreneurial.'" Mason added, "It was through no ambition of my own that any of this happened." With $1 million from Lefkofsky, Mason again left school to see his new project through.

"MAKE SOMETHING HAPPEN"

The Point's slogan was "Make something happen. More than a petition. Better than a fundraiser." The site first launched in November 2007. At first, Mason was very idealistic about it; he thought it could be a tool to change the world for the better. Among the site users' first prominent efforts was a campaign to force KFC, the fried chicken fast-food chain, to treat animals more humanely. The Point users also urged Pepsi-Cola and other food and beverage products to switch to biodegradable containers.

Despite its enormous potential for social activism, the Point had lower-than-expected subscriptions. Mason needed to make it financially viable if he wanted to keep it afloat. Some of the projects launched using the Point collected money, and Mason and his team took small percentages of these donations. Yet many of the Point's users were anticorporate activists and other socially conscious campaigners. They operated on a shoestring budget, were not-for-profit, or were merely getting the word out rather than raising money. This kind of clientele did not provide a very healthy revenue stream. As a result, Mason was unable to support himself full-time with the Point, and he was unable to provide any profits to his investors.

CHAPTER 2

Let's Make a Deal! The Early Days of Groupon

The seeds of what would one day become Groupon had been planted early. With Andrew Mason's work ethic, desire to try new things, and technological savvy, it seemed almost certain that he was on the road to breakout, high-profile success. But it would take a few tries before one of his ventures not only got off the ground but also remained airborne. Mason's next project went through a couple of revisions and trips back to the drawing board. It benefited from able leadership and was lucky enough to land in the right place at the right time. Little did Mason or anyone else know just how big it would be.

OUT OF THE ASHES: A NEW DIRECTION

Mason set up a subsidiary of the Point that concentrated on commerce rather than political and social issues. He had noticed that the most popular campaigns on the site had actually involved people getting together into groups to purchase something and/or take advantage of some deal. This seemed to be a more popular activity than mobilizing fellow users for organized collective action on some issue of the day.

Mason realized that commerce, shopping, and bargains should have been the primary focus of the Point all along. His mentor, Lefkofsky, highly encouraged this change in direction. Far from feeling discouraged about his miscalculation and the Point's subsequent lackluster performance, Mason simply decided to brush himself off and get back up again, in a better position than ever before. During a speech to a technology group (as quoted by the *Pittsburgh Post-Gazette*), Mason claimed, "The biggest mistake we made with the Point was…making assumptions about what people want. You [discover] you are way too dumb to figure out what people want."

Mason was not necessarily calling himself or his staff dumb. Rather, he was pointing out a valuable lesson in being overconfident or arrogant in your belief that you know your audience or users and their wants and needs. Sometimes you just have to listen to what they say they want and need and closely observe their behavior when using your service. How visitors were using the Point should have told Mason everything he needed to know about what they wanted from the site. Rather than persist in believing that they would want to use it to organize social action, he came to accept that discounted goods and services were what his users were really after. As a result, the side project of the Point was now poised to become Mason's flagship, or main project.

GROUPON IS BORN

For his new commerce-based subsidiary of the Point, Mason coined the name "Groupon" along with his coworker Aaron With (now editor in chief of Groupon). They combined the words "group" and "coupon." The mash-up word, Groupon, combines the concept of collective action that characterized the Point and the new emphasis on the purchasing of discounted goods and services. Initially, Mason thought the subsidiary would just help pay the bills and subsidize the Point's operations. He didn't expect Groupon to become the star of the show.

Groupon was launched in November 2008. Its first offer to the public was a two-for-one deal on pizza from the Motel Bar, the bar/restaurant located on the ground floor of Groupon's Chicago office. Twenty-four Chicagoans took advantage of the half-off discount.

Since this modest beginning, Groupon's offers have changed somewhat, and the company has refined its business model a number of times. But its basic service remains the same. Every morning, a "deal of the day" is advertised on the site. Registered users receive the deal via e-mail, text message, and other forms of digital delivery. The deal of the day might be a 70 percent discount

Aaron With, Groupon's editor in chief and a longtime associate of Andrew Mason, is pictured busy at work overseeing editorial staff at Groupon's Chicago headquarters. As Groupon expands, With and others must balance rapid growth with the maintenance of high editorial standards.

on a meal at a popular local restaurant. But the deal can only be claimed if enough users respond and purchase the deal coupon. When the target number of users respond, the deal is triggered—in other words, Groupon's users reach the "tipping point" that the Point also relied on to mobilize collective action. In fact, Groupon's staff usually refer to that number as the point at which the deal "tips."

Groupon and the participating restaurant (or other retail establishment offering goods or services) both make money if the deal is a success. Assuming that the user who buys the coupon would not have otherwise eaten at that restaurant on that day, the restaurant makes money that it wouldn't have made if it hadn't offered the discounted meal. So if a Groupon-advertised meal would normally cost $60 but is being offered for $20, the restaurant makes $10 that it wouldn't have made if it hadn't offered the discount. (Groupon gets the other $10; most deals are structured so that Groupon and the business split the deal revenue 50/50.)

In addition, businesses that make deals with Groupon hope to build a loyal clientele that will return, even if and when the goods and services aren't being discounted. It is not yet clear, however, if partnering with Groupon does indeed lead to repeat customers for businesses, or if Groupon users simply chase the deals and avoid any non-discounted goods and services.

A NEW MARKETING MODEL

Groupon insists that even if a restaurant or other kind of retail establishment doesn't make a tremendous amount of money when offering a Groupon deal, it still wins potential new customers who are likely to return again and pay full price. Plus, the customers who come in with a Groupon coupon may be so delighted by the discount that they will spend a little extra—by ordering dessert and coffee, for example. Even when spending extra, they still feel like they are saving money and getting a deal. Altogether, according to Mason at least, partnering with Groupon on deals is a "win-win-win" situation for the merchant, Groupon, and its users.

In some ways, there is little risk to businesses in partnering with Groupon, especially those that are looking to increase their customer base. It costs them nothing to offer a deal. If the deal doesn't tip—if not enough people buy the coupon to activate it—the deal simply dies. In such a case, there is no financial penalty or loss to the business. If it does tip, the business gains customers who will buy products or services that would probably otherwise go unsold. The business stands to make more money than it otherwise would, even though it is offering its goods and services at a discount. The deal can create goodwill with customers, who will then be more inclined to return, with or without a Groupon coupon.

Attracting new customers—or former customers who have not returned in a while—can be much cheaper this way than attempting to bring in more business through traditional forms of advertising. There is no cost to the merchant for offering the deal—unless it tips, and then, of course, Groupon and the merchant split the money earned. Because of this, Groupon's team considers their model a great alternative to traditional advertising. Normally, a business pays to broadcast its commercial on television or the radio, or to place ads in a newspaper or magazine. Online advertising has also grown in

Naomi Reyolds (*right*), a Groupon user, hands her Groupon deal printout to Jesse Layman, executive chef and general manager of the Modesto, California-based eatery Galletto Ristorante for a half-price discount on her meal.

popularity. But there is no guarantee that any of these efforts will bring in any business at all. Mason told Mixergy.com that many businesses—especially smaller, local ones—take a big chance in devoting money to online advertising. Its effectiveness is not at all proven despite its expense. "I think with business owners, [it was] critical… finding a way to take all the risk out of being online."

One can see how Groupon's model would be very appealing to many business owners, not to mention their customers. Mason felt it was very important to make the process simple for users and, in each daily deal, clearly show them what they were getting in exchange for buying a Groupon coupon. As Mason put it to *Chicago* magazine, the daily deal is a "dead-simple value that you can comprehend by looking at one page in three seconds."

GETTING THE LAY OF THE LAND

Groupon's sales teams often have several weeks to research and explore a new city or locality that the company is considering doing business in. This usually means getting a large list of possible contacts, including a wide variety of merchants that might be interested in working with Groupon. As the company has gained popularity, its reputation has preceded it. In its earlier days, it would have to reach out to many more businesses. These days, it has a waiting list of merchants trying to get in on the action.

Still, Groupon won't partner with just anybody. Part of the sales teams' research is checking popular online review sites like Yelp or CitySearch, local newspapers and magazines, and other media to make sure that certain businesses are well established and well regarded. It also targets lesser-known businesses, which can benefit greatly from the sudden huge push and publicity of a daily deal. Sales teams then reach out to the business owners to explain how Groupon works. This is now easier due to the company's exploding popularity. But it is still necessary to negotiate the terms of the deal and respond to any of the merchants' questions or concerns.

Meanwhile, Groupon's marketing team, separate from but working closely with the sales department, will promote the company's imminent arrival in the neighborhood, city, or locality. Depending on the area, the marketers may use traditional print or online advertising. They may also get the word out through social networks like Facebook, Twitter, and Foursquare.

GROUPON'S FIRST YEAR

From its first discounted pizza deal made downstairs from its Chicago offices, Groupon rapidly expanded. It started operations with a staff of only a few dozen people. Soon, it opened offices in other U.S. cities. Among the first were Boston and New York. Within its first year of operation, Groupon expanded operations into more than twenty-four U.S. cities, including large urban markets like San Francisco, Seattle, and Washington, D.C. By the fall of 2009, Mason indicated that 750,000 people had cashed in nearly 400,000 Groupon coupons.

Especially successful early deals included a New York spa offering two massages for $75 (normally a $150 purchase). The tipping point for this deal was a minimum of sixty people. Ultimately, about a thousand people took advantage of the offer.

For many businesses, setting up shop toward the end of 2008 might have seemed like a foolish move. The U.S. and global economies were entering one of the worst recessions—or business slowdowns—in decades. Millions of jobs were lost, and even people who had some money were more likely to pinch pennies.

However, Mason saw it as the ideal time to start operations. People were hungrier for deals in the sour economy. Despite the prolonged recession, many still wanted to make luxury and leisure purchase . They wanted to purchase a nice meal, spa treatment, or theater tickets, but they could not—or would not—pay top dollar.

Mason also enjoyed appealing to Groupon users' sense of adventure, their desire to take chances on new experiences. This was especially true for things they might not have tried because they may have been a bit too expensive to risk their money on without a Groupon coupon in hand. "Part of the fun of this business is sending a deal that is for something

Groupon Discount Offers... and Free Chuckles

- "Because baseball games are no longer used to settle land disputes and damages from horse collisions, they've become the battleground for deciding which U.S. city will be the first to move to the moon. Catch a nation-changing showdown with today's GrouponLive deal for a lower-reserved outfield ticket and admission to a two-hour pregame patio party, which includes a barbecue buffet and drinks, at a Chicago White Sox game at U.S. Cellular Field." (Groupon Chicago)

- "Having sore muscles, like signing a five-year lease or wearing lead socks, makes it difficult to move. Evict tense muscles with today's Groupon to Inner Peace Holistic Center." (Groupon Cincinnati)

- "Many theatergoers claim that life imitates art, which can be frustrating when they pause arguments for intermissions or direct drivers to turn 'stage left' at stop signs. Learn to navigate the theatrical world with today's GrouponLive deal to Des Moines Community Playhouse." (Groupon Des Moines, Iowa) you normally don't do, like getting a deal to go to an indoor rock-climbing facility or experience a sensory-deprivation tank," Mason told AOL Small Business in August 2010.

He felt gratified knowing that, from a person's use of Groupon, he or she may have gained a new hobby in rock-climbing, fallen in love with a new kind of food, or gained a new appreciation for opera or classical music. The last thing Mason wanted was to follow the traditional path of a "typical" CEO or entrepreneur and have everything be simply about the money. Coming from a creative background, he envisioned bringing an artistic sensibility to any moneymaking endeavor. Otherwise, he predicted that he would grow bored and frustrated.

EXPLOSIVE GROWTH

With a combination of profits and venture capital funding, Groupon grew faster than any other Internet company before it. (Venture capital firms are companies that pump money into new businesses in the hopes that they can make much more money down the line.) This included big-name, hugely successful firms like eBay, Amazon, Yahoo!, AOL, and Google. It had reached a $1 billion market valuation quicker than any other profitable company in history. According to *Forbes*, Groupon had an estimated value of about $1.35 billion by April 2010. At the time, only the mighty YouTube had grown more quickly (though, unlike Groupon, it had not made a profit at the time it hit $1 billion).

Groupon deals extend to nearly every service imaginable. Here, young singles gather to break the world speed-dating record. This was a contest coorganized by Groupon New York and SingleIntheCity.com, in which users received dating services ordinarily valued at $100 for only $32.

As it grew, Groupon attracted the attention not just of local merchants, but also of national retailers, institutions, and multinational corporations. As a result, it partnered up with more and more companies. The number, size, and prominence of the deals grew significantly. In May 2010, for example, the Discovery Channel's King Tut exhibit in New York City's Times Square teamed up with Groupon. In a day, Groupon sold 6,561 tickets to the exhibit for $18 each, about half price. Another big win that same month was a boat tour that explored the architecture of downtown Chicago. It took only eight hours to sell 19,822 Groupon tickets at $12 a ticket (normally priced at $25). Groupon and the tour operator divided the resulting revenue of $238,000.

In August 2010, Groupon again received media coverage for a nationwide deal with the Gap, the biggest deal of its kind to date. Through Groupon, the retailer offered $50 worth of clothing and other products for only $25. By the end of the day, the traffic was so heavy for the 441,000 Groupon coupons that were eventually sold that the deal crashed Groupon's Web site. This marked the first time that Groupon strayed from its model of providing highly local deals in favor of a national offer with a chain-store partner.

CHAPTER 3

Inside Groupon: Mixing Business and Art

As Groupon began to make waves as the newest online sensation, the public began to become acquainted with Andrew Mason, its eccentric and humorous chief executive officer (CEO) and founder.

Mason set out to create a corporate culture in which people would be encouraged to excel in their jobs while always approaching the work with a strong sense of humor and creativity. In his words, Groupon employees were "mixing business and art." He wanted the office environment to be lighthearted, comical, and even a bit strange. He also wanted Groupon's deal offers to reflect this adventurous, fun-loving, and witty perspective. Many users of Groupon find enormous entertainment value in the text of the offers, whether or not they purchase the coupons.

At the same time, Mason realized that hard work and rapid expansion would be necessary if Groupon were to remain viable, flourish, and endure. The class clown within him would have to join forces with the workaholic. Groupon would not take itself too seriously. But the untapped daily deals market—soon to grow incredibly competitive—would be a very serious game indeed, with increasingly high stakes.

ANDREW MASON: PERSONALITY TO SPARE

Mason has made plenty of headlines since coming into the public eye. Aside from the incredible growth and success of Groupon, he has gained a reputation for being a prankster in the office. In addition, he has also attempted to portray himself as someone who avoids approaching things in a conservative or traditionally corporate way. In fact, a substantial portion of the media coverage of Groupon has focused upon Mason's sometimes outlandish stories and sense of humor.

Questioned about his official bio on Groupon's Web site, Mason gave an interviewer the truth about whether he actually did own twenty cats (one of the claims in the bio). "No," he told CNBC. "Most CEOs will make stuff up about themselves to sound way smarter and cooler, and people are disappointed to find out otherwise. I decided to set the bar very low and make up lies about myself that make me sound lame."

Demonstrating Groupon's sense of humor (and his own), Andrew Mason listens to music while pedaling a stationary bike in "Michael's Room." This room is the supposed residence of a fictional resident of the Groupon offices who plays occasional harmless pranks during working hours.

Mason's irreverence about his public persona sometimes appears comical, but it has certainly worked to keep him—and Groupon—in the news. He realizes that so many initially successful companies (and CEOs) have suffered from unrealistic expectations. One of their mistakes, he feared, was taking themselves too seriously and letting money and attention fool them into thinking they were invincible.

Andrew Mason on Groupon's Culture

"The way people think about jobs, the nine to five… it's the same routine over and over again. Groupon as a company…is about surprise. A new deal that surprises you every day. We've carried that over to our brand, in the writing and the marketing…and in the internal corporate culture."
—*Wall Street Journal*, **December 20, 2010**

"Our philosophy isn't to tell jokes; it's to surprise people."
—*Pittsburgh Post-Gazette*, **November 14, 2010**

This was especially true during the era of the dot-com bubble and its catastrophic aftermath and the later Web 2.0 age. For instance, social networks once considered industry leaders and pioneers, like Friendster and MySpace, were eventually overtaken and surpassed by Facebook. Meanwhile, enduring companies like eBay, Yahoo!, Google, and Amazon have outpaced many of their other rivals that once seemed poised for great success but ultimately fizzled out.

"DON'T BE BORING"

Google, perhaps one of the most successful Internet companies ever, has a semiofficial slogan: "Don't Be Evil." If Groupon had an official company slogan, it might be: "Don't Be Boring." Mason's sometimes eccentric interviews, personal

Casually dressed Groupon employees, some of them enjoying music while busy at work, are shown at the company's Chicago offices. A dry-erase board displayed behind them allows employees to get their creative juices flowing.

claims, and prankish behavior in the office have gained his company the reputation of being a fun and dynamic one to work for.

From its very beginnings, Groupon prided itself on its nontraditional corporate culture. "As the company grows and the external pressures to conform become greater, it's more and more tempting for us not to conform," Mason told the *Chicago Tribune*. This perspective on how to do business differs from the traditional corporate culture, where people must dress formally and work in more conventional ways. He repeated this mantra to *Vanity Fair*, saying, "As we get bigger, instead of being like most companies, conforming and becoming more normal, we want to become weirder."

With these goals of nonconformity in mind, the youthful and irreverent attitude that Mason has tried to instill grows out of his own experience. In 2012, Mason himself was only thirty-one—very young for a CEO of a billion-dollar company. Much of Groupon's staff is also young. Many are in their twenties and thirties, with the average age being twenty-five. Groupon continues to attract fresh talent as the company expands both in the United States and internationally. Its staff includes many creative people—writers, artists, designers, and comedians, among others.

Chicago is known for its creative talent. Its abundance of technology companies, universities, newspapers and other publishing and media firms and its famous tradition of comedy (including improv, or improvisational comedy) makes it a great place for Groupon to recruit new workers. In addition, Mason and much of upper management actively seek out creative people for many staff positions. Director of Communications Julie Mossler told public radio station WBEZ in May 2011: "[Being] a comedian or an artist is a selling point for certain roles at Groupon… We've found that improv actors are usually quite empathetic, think quickly, and really connect with customers, making them perfect customer service representatives. Writers and artists are woven into the fabric of Groupon's culture…they keep the company colorful."

Mason's own creative publicity stunts, pranks, and other very "uncorporate" behavior set the tone at Groupon. Employees are attracted to the company's in-house culture: no dress code and no official vacation policy. Employees are given a lot of personal autonomy (freedom), and many can make their own schedules. Freed from the traditional nine-to-five hours, creative people in the arts have flocked to Groupon.

Former college classmate and bandmate (and now employee) Andrew With made clear to MSNBC that

Mason, despite his personality, "runs the show like he did the music—smart and driven—but with a very weird sense of humor about the whole experience." For example, employees were treated early on to the sight of a man hired by Mason to walk around the offices dressed in a ballerina's tutu, for a week straight, without speaking to anyone.

Much of this off-the-wall behavior, while amusing, serves a real business purpose, according to colleagues and employees. Mason entertains himself, even as he stays focused on the hard work and goals that keep him going as CEO. His delicate mix of business and art energizes both himself and his employees. The pranks and stunts, and many of the humorous props and items found in Groupon's offices are all part of Mason's efforts to stimulate creativity, humor, and fresh perspectives in his employees. They serve to break up the boring, creativity-stifling drudgery that many office workers at other companies experience.

"THE WRITE STUFF"

One of the most important components of Groupon's team is the editorial staff. While building its Chicago operation, Groupon took advantage of the large pool of talent available in the creative metropolitan area. Mason started with a team of about seven people. Everyone participated in calling up new local businesses to ask them if they wanted to partner with the daily deals.

Since these early days, the basic business model and pitch to retail partners have remained the same, according to Mason. He told Mixergy.com, "We've gotten more refined and efficient at doing it, but it's still figuring out how to explain this new concept to people. The best way to describe it is, 'If we can get a ton of new customers to your store, will you give us a great price?'"

By May 2011, Groupon had more than four hundred people working as editors and writers. As the business has grown, Mason has attracted teams of writers who work to make the deals not only clear and attractive to users, but entertaining, too. A whole team of writers might

A Groupon employee is busy at work in his cubicle, decorated with a humorous sign and a Mexican sombrero. Individuality, creativity, and a fun work environment are some of the things that Andrew Mason hopes to maintain as Groupon continues to expand.

go through the copy (or written content) of a particular deal before it is posted that day. One reason for such high standards is to keep customers interested. A user might take advantage of a daily deal one week and then not buy another one for several weeks or months. Mason claims that many customers return regularly simply to read the deals, even if they do not take advantage of them.

Hence, one of the most important things is keeping "the voice" of Groupon fresh and lively. This includes the writing of the daily deals, the management bios on the Web site, and its general corporate approach that's rooted in intelligent, and sometimes bizarre, humor.

Andrew With, Groupon's editor in chief and Mason's former bandmate, has been with the company from the very beginning. He oversees the editorial staff, including the stable of writers. He claims that many Groupon users make enough money that cheap meals are not the only factor in determining whether or not they buy a coupon. Sometimes it is the way the deal is offered that tips the balance. When a deal is presented in a smart, humorous, and creative manner, readers are more likely to commit to it. They will keep returning to check out more deals for the entertainment value of the ad copy, if not the promise of discounted goods and services. "People have grown numb to the elements of advertising that pander to their fears and hopes, that insult their intelligence with safe, bland approaches at creativity...We're mixing business with art and creating our own voice," With told the *New York Times*.

Groupon's unique approach uses creative copy to appeal to its clientele's intelligence and sense of adventure. In the process, the company has created an entirely fresh and unique consumer experience.

MASON'S INNER CIRCLE

Groupon has many things going for it: a billion-dollar idea; the creativity, intelligence, and dedication of a one-of-a-kind CEO; and an enthusiastic, witty, and dedicated staff. As it grew rapidly, the company required executives who were as unique and committed as Mason and his staff to supporting and managing the rapid growth. Since launching, Groupon has benefited from the collective talent and experience of not only its original backers, like Lefkofsky, but also handpicked and seasoned veterans. Mason's inner circle boasts a top-notch roster of Internet business figures.

One of the most important executives in any large company is the chief financial officer (CFO). Though CFOs can do many things, they are generally responsible for keeping track of the company's money, including spending and profits. They are often copartners with CEOs in planning company growth.

In December 2010, Groupon selected Jason Child as its CFO. Child was hired after a twelve-year stint as vice president of finance for the international division of Internet retail giant Amazon. During that time, he handled a $14 billion business. He had all-around skills, international experience, and previous roles in marketing and investor relations. This made Child a natural choice to enable Groupon to expand worldwide and eventually go public. "Going public" is when a previously privately owned company begins selling ownership shares—or stocks—to the general public. Google went public in November 2011.

Not long after Groupon turned down Google in its 2010 acquisition bid (see chapter 4), it made its own acquisitions: it lured away two Google executives to join its team. These hires, along with Child and others, made observers comment that Groupon seemed to be getting serious about a possible initial public offering (IPO) in the near future. Mason seemed poised to go public.

The first of these high-profile hires was Jason Harinstein, who joined Groupon in March 2011 as senior vice president of corporate development. Harinstein had been director of corporate development at Google. He had helped the search giant make some big-time purchases and develop new business as head of its mergers and acquisitions team.

Groupon made headlines again when it signed on Margo Georgiadis as its new chief operating officer (COO) the following month. This put Georgiadis in charge of the company's global sales, marketing, and operations. She had headed Google's global sales operations. Georgiadis replaced Rob Solomon, a former Yahoo! executive who left after only a year at Groupon. Some wondered if Solomon simply did not feel that he was the right one to lead the company in its incredible growth, while others believed he might have had differences with the unpredictable and eccentric Mason.

Similar questions were raised again when Georgiadis also quickly resigned at Groupon. In September 2011, she returned to Google after only five months with Mason's company. Her parting comments were designed to dampen any speculation about dissatisfaction with Groupon, its corporate culture, or future prospects. "Groupon is a great company and I feel privileged to have worked there, even for a short time," she wrote. "It was a hard decision to leave as the company is on a terrific path. I have complete confidence in the team's ability to realize its mission" (as quoted by the *Chicago Tribune*). Mason, on the other hand, stated that, in terms of hiring, "It would have been great if I could say that we batted 1,000 percent, but that's rarely the case."

Georgiadis had years of experience in investment, marketing, and retail operations, among many other areas. Her hiring had been met with much industry approval. It seemed to signal that Groupon was getting serious about the business side of things, even if its corporate culture was still characterized by a loose sense of fun and adventure. Her rapid departure shook many peoples' confidence in Mason, Groupon, and the company's long-term viability. Yet Mason vowed that he would find just the right combination of players and continue to assemble his daily deals "A-Team," so to speak. Or, in Groupon terms, "G-Team."

Groupon's Unbelievable Bios

If you come across the bios for Mason's team on the Groupon Web site, take the content there with a grain of salt. Much of it is a good-natured joke. For example, Brian Totty does not have "advanced degrees in bodybuilding." Nor did Margo Georgiadis ensure that her name appeared first in every Internet search while working at Google. While it is true that Aaron Cooper "had heard of more than five musical instruments," it is untrue that Jason Child has skied Austria's toughest mountain "with his wife and two children strapped to his back." It is also doubtful that Andrew Mason is writing a book called *Unleash the Power Within the Power Within: Self-Help for Self-Helpers*. Visit the Senior Management page of Groupon's site for a few more chuckles.

THE REST OF THE "G-TEAM"

Mason's other top people are also well regarded in their fields. Aaron Cooper is currently the senior vice president of customer marketing. Before Groupon, he was an executive vice president of marketing at optionsXpress, a financial services company, and handled online marketing for the travel site Orbitz.

Heading product management as senior vice president, Jeff Holden was picked for his extensive background developing software and heading software development teams. He had many roles at Amazon and later cofounded the Seattle-based company Pelago. This company developed a location-based, geosocial application game called Whrrl that helps users explore their neighborhoods, cities, and localities. Groupon bought Pelago in April 2011. Holden said at the time that combining Whrrl's resources with Groupon's similar desire to get users to take chances on new local experiences at a discount made the acquisition a natural fit.

Vice president of product, David Jesse, came from Gaia Online. This site ran an anime-based online world/social networking platform. Jesse was previously a veteran of eBay.

Ron "Skip" Schipper is the head of global human resources (HR) for the company. He previously spent a few years heading the HR department of the computer

A creative team handling a Groupon project—known internally as "Black Cat Wearing a Gold Nameplate Necklace"—includes, from left, designer Dav Yandler and writers Wes Haney, Cullen Crawford, and Daniel Kibblesmith. They are brainstorming ideas for the whimsically code-named project at Groupon's Chicago offices.

networking giant Cisco Systems, which has more than seventy thousand employees.

Before becoming Groupon's senior VP of sales, Darren Schwartz was, like Mason, an entrepreneur, starting and running SureSpeak. This Chicago-based company created and sold a platform that helped users improve sales, presentation, and general communication skills.

Finally, Brian Totty leads the engineering team as senior VP. Totty worked at Apple and several other high-tech firms, researching and developing Internet and multimedia technology. He also used his vast knowledge of computer science as an educator and an author of a book on computing.

Despite the rapid departures of COOs Solomon and Georgiadis, it is clear to many business analysts that Groupon has gathered an accomplished team, bringing together a wide range of experience in the fields of technology and the Web. The management that Mason assembled has helped convince many that Groupon is serious about its daily deals business becoming an undisputed and enduring e-commerce industry leader and not just another bright, but brief, dot-com flameout.

CHAPTER 4

Valuing Groupon

In Groupon's June 2011 Securities and Exchange Commission (SEC) filing, it estimated that it had more than 3,500 employees working as part of its sales force. (All companies, foreign and domestic, are required to periodically file financial reports with this federal government regulatory agency.) Groupon's sales representatives were spread out over 175 markets in North American and in 43 countries.

The sales force plays a large part in Groupon's expansion into new domestic and international markets. Thanks largely to these men and women, Groupon's assets were valued at $225 million, and its second-quarter revenue for 2011 was $878,018,000. As of June 2011, the company employed 9,625 people and boasted approximately 115,000,000 users. It was operating in 45 countries and 565 cities.

GOOGLE GOES FOR GROUPON

In late 2010, Groupon was riding high and thus had become a tempting target of companies hoping to acquire it for their own. On November 30, 2010, Google made a $6 billion offer to buy Groupon. This was nearly twice as much as Google had ever paid for any of the many companies it had purchased over the years. For example, it had bought DoubleClick for only $3.1 billion in 2007. This had to have been a very tempting offer for Mason. He and the Groupon team stood to gain amazing wealth almost overnight if they agreed. However, Mason passed on the deal.

Scott Munro, a partner at venture capital company Pagemill Partners, saw the decision as Groupon signaling

From its Mountain View headquarters in northern California's famed Silicon Valley, Google, Inc. continues to expand and may prove to be a formidable daily deals challenger to Groupon. Google's 2010 offer to buy Groupon was rejected by Mason.

that it thought it could get even bigger. He told *Time* in February 2011, "Very few companies can emerge like Facebook has…[Groupon] must know something that I don't know to turn down that amount of dough."

Competition on the Web has always been fierce. Companies often buy other companies they see as the "next big thing." Sometimes they acquire companies they regard as competition. Purchasing competing companies removes the threat, and many of the purchased companies get quietly absorbed or shut down. Such acquisitions can be great successes or great failures. Previously popular companies might crash and burn after a merger or acquisition. Others receive a jolt of new life, an infusion of cash, and far greater visibility and prominence. The decision whether to make an offer—or take one—is often difficult.

For example, Friendster turned down an offer from Google and soon faded away as Facebook came to dominate the online social networking scene. On the other hand, companies that Google purchased have not always done well after their new parent company attempted to change how they operated. Mason may have feared Google's interference in its unique operations, business model, and corporate culture. Whatever the reasons, he decided to keep going his own way and forge his own vision for Groupon. Mason wanted to remain unhindered by any higher-up looking over his shoulder, calling the shots, and questioning or overruling his decisions.

AN AWKWARD MATCH: TECHNOLOGY VS. "THE HUMAN TOUCH"

Whether Mason's gamble against a deal with Google was brilliant or a "Friendster fumble" remains to be seen. Part of his reluctance to sell was that he wanted to preserve Groupon's corporate culture and maintain the company's independence.

Some commentators believe that Groupon and Google would not have fit well together, given how different their business cultures and methods are. Venturebeat's Owen Thomas wrote in November 2010, prior to the Google offer: "There's an ongoing debate over whether Groupon would have thrived in Silicon Valley [unofficial headquarters of the U.S. technology industry], with [Silicon Valley's] emphasis on computer servers over customer service." For Thomas and others, Groupon is a company with more of a "human touch," with technology not being a primary factor in its success. This is in contrast to Google, which has risen due to its expertise in programming and creating sophisticated algorithms for the purposes of searches and marketing.

Though no deal was made, Google's offer for Groupon made many people take notice, especially those unfamiliar with Mason's daily deals. In the following weeks, Groupon added three million subscribers, thanks largely to the Google-related publicity. It also announced that it had raised $950 million through a number of venture capital and investment firms to help expand its operations, possibly in advance of an IPO. The infusion of investment dollars would make Groupon be valued higher if it went public, meaning its share prices would also be higher. Higher share prices mean Groupon would make more money when it began selling shares after going public.

GOING PUBLIC?

In June 2011, it was announced that Groupon had filed for an IPO. This would transform it from a private business, owned by Mason and his partners, to a public one owned by shareholders. In an IPO, some or all of the company is sold to new investors in the form of shares of stock. Many companies go public to raise more money to grow the business and make a lot of money for the owners and/or original investors.

In order to have a successful IPO, Mason and his partners needed to prove to the stock-buying public that Groupon was in good shape and had strong prospects for future growth. The company, which had grown and earned money very quickly, also had to show that its success would continue, both in the near future and in the long run.

To begin the process of an IPO, Groupon had to file an "S1" form with the SEC, which makes and enforces the rules for how public companies should behave. This public filing allows potential investors and shareholders (those hoping to buy stock when Groupon goes public) a chance to "look under the hood" of Groupon.

As detailed in the S1 filing, by August 2011, Groupon, though only in business for less than three years, had impressive numbers. With more than 7,100 employees, it had achieved earnings of $713 million in 2010, with a profit of $61 million. Its earnings for the first quarter (first three months) of 2011 were about $82 million.

The Washington, D.C., headquarters of the Securities and Exchange Commission (SEC) is pictured here. Groupon was compelled to satisfy the SEC's strict guidelines on reporting financial numbers in order to successfully file for its IPO.

However, some critics and analysts didn't feel these numbers told the whole truth. In its SEC filing, Groupon used "adjusted consolidated segment operating income," or ACSOI for short. In plain English, it did not include certain "overhead" costs—the money spent to grow the company and run the business. These unreported overhead costs included money spent to buy competitors, enter new markets around the world, and register new users. Some financial observers claimed that if these costs were factored in, they would show that Groupon had actually lost money in its three years of operation and never turned a profit.

Some defenders of Groupon assert that many now-successful businesses, especially Web-based ones, only become profitable after several years of operation. Groupon stated that it had to spend a lot of money early on in order to sign up users. It claimed the solid and loyal base of users that it had built up would soon begin to make it profitable.

Others argued that it was too early for Groupon's IPO, saying it should show much healthier earnings versus spending before offering ownership shares. Some commentators suspected the venture capital firms that invested in Groupon, as well as Mason and his partners, were simply looking to "flip" their investment as fast as they could. This means they were hoping to get Groupon valued as highly as possible—whether or not the high valuation was truly justified. They would then make a killing

Mason: Too Off-the-Wall?

Andrew Mason's corporate style may be one of the factors leading to a lower valuation for his company and its stock. On the one hand, many of Groupon's employees—current and prospective ones—are attracted to his unconventional leadership. However, when it comes to Wall Street and the stock market, this freewheeling, high-spirited style could backfire. People investing large amounts of money want to put it in a sure thing. They are looking for a company that is well governed and seriously committed to making the difficult decisions and ruthless moves necessary to ensure growth and competitiveness. Mason's unpredictable statements and behavior might scare away more conservative investors.

Despite its enormous early success, Groupon still had to prove itself in the days leading up to its IPO and even beyond. As *Wall Street Journal* blogger Scott Austin put it, "[But] once Groupon goes public, everything will be placed under a magnifying glass, and Mason will constantly need to defend his company."

by selling high-priced shares in the company and more than recouping their own earlier investment in Groupon.

When it first announced its intention to have an IPO, market analysts guessed that Groupon could end up being valued at between $20 billion and $30 billion. They believed it could possibly even outdo Google's 2004 IPO, which had that company valued at about $24 billion.

When Groupon publicly adjusted its accounting numbers in response to critics of its SEC filing, it became unclear if the company's valuation would reach $20 billion after all. Some analysts estimated its likely value at closer to $14.5 billion. Ultimately, Groupon was valued at $12.8 billion before its first day of public trading in November 2011. Each share was initially sold for $20. On the first day of trading Groupon shares rose 31 percent from that level to $28, valuing the company at $16.7 billion. Only three weeks later, however, share prices had plummeted to $15.24.

ATTACK OF THE "CLONES"?

Another factor in the valuation of Groupon is the increasing competition that it is beginning to experience in the online discount field. It was not unique in its business model, even in its earliest days. Other companies in the United States and abroad had similar ideas for merchant coupons, while others blatantly copied what Groupon was doing. Mason and his team knew that they would have to stay one step ahead of the ever-growing competition, all over the world. Otherwise, they risked losing ground and becoming irrelevant.

Yelp is an influential review site for goods and services, including restaurants and retailers. Yelp reviews have helped Groupon figure out which merchants to partner with, even as Yelp itself launched its own competing daily deals service in mid-2010.

In a private memo to employees, later leaked to the *Wall Street Journal*, Mason reminded them that they could not rest, even though they were currently riding the success of a great idea. "Not only must we continue to beat the thousands of clones who lifted our idea and began at roughly the same time as we did," he warned, "but now we must also beat the biggest, smartest technology companies in the world." He was referring to new challengers in the online discount game, including giants like Google and Facebook.

CHAPTER 5

Growing Pains and Hard Lessons

When a company is the leader in its industry or field, there are plenty of others that hope to knock it off its perch and take its place. Groupon has been especially vulnerable to this kind of reversal due to fierce competition, growing pains, flaws in its business model, and some very public setbacks.

SIZING UP THE COMPETITION

Though Groupon is the clear leader of the pack, it has a growing number of serious competitors. Some of its smaller competitors are BuyWithMe, OpenTable, Travelzoo, YouSwoop, and Scoop St. But its main threat thus far is the Washington, D.C.-based daily deal site Living-Social. LivingSocial was originally a producer of services such as Facebook applications. It entered the daily deal game in 2009 and quickly grew to be the number two player in the field.

LivingSocial's deals are similar to Groupon's. The primary difference is that its users earn the discounts by getting other people to sign on with LivingSocial and use its services. It also has a more specialized service for travel-related discounts. A LivingSocial travel deal might not be half price, but it may include free meals and many other extras specially tailored to the customer.

LivingSocial has not expanded with quite the astonishing speed that Groupon has, but it has still experienced rapid growth. Groupon usually offers bigger discounts—between 50 and 90 percent off the usual price for the good or service versus LivingSocial's standard 50

A LivingSocial employee displays the company's smartphone app in New York City during its "dollar lunch day" promotion. This is one of many tactics Groupon's main competitor has employed to catch up with and surpass the market leader.

percent. Yet many LivingSocial users claim that the deals and the goods and services offered are of a higher quality. Many retailers have also expressed greater pleasure in working with LivingSocial than with Groupon.

Industry pioneer Steve Case, the founder of AOL, has invested in LivingSocial, and the site has also received strong support from powerful online retailer Amazon. Various other venture capital firms have also invested to the point that the company was reportedly valued at about $3 billion as of April 2011.

LivingSocial is not Groupon's biggest competitive threat, however. Having failed to acquire Groupon, Google decided to compete with it directly. It was leaked in early 2011 that Google would launch Google Offers, its own daily deal service. Unlike Groupon, Google Offers would provide discounts on goods and services regardless of how many people opted to sign on for a particular deal. There would be no need to achieve a tipping point before a deal became activated.

Starting in Portland, Oregon, Google Offers recently launched in New York and San Francisco. Time will tell how successful the service will be and whether it will successfully challenge Groupon's model.

GROUPON GOES OVERSEAS

In its constant effort to grow and gain a competitive edge, Groupon began looking overseas for new consumer markets to enter. In May 2010, it scored a big win when it purchased CityDeal, a major European player in the daily deals market. Founded in December 2009, CityDeal was one of many Groupon clones that had sprung up in Germany that year, and it became the largest and most popular. With this acquisition, Groupon gained the German firm's eighty already-established markets, spanning sixteen European countries. Eventually, all of CityDeal's Web sites and markets came under the Groupon name, including England's MyCityDeal.

Just before this European expansion, Groupon had received $135 million from Moscow-based Digital Sky Technologies, a Russian venture capital and investment firm. This infusion of Russian funds allowed Groupon to purchase Darberry, the Russian version of Groupon, and Qpod, the Japanese daily deals company, in August 2010. From 165 markets in 18 countries, Groupon jumped to 230 markets in 29 countries with the stroke of a pen. Less than two years after launching in Chicago, Groupon was a global force that seemed increasingly unbeatable.

COURTING CONTROVERSY

By early 2011, a few public relations stumbles occurred that demonstrated that Groupon was not invincible or infallible after all. One of the company's most prominent early setbacks occurred during its push into Asian markets.

Scooping Groupon Down Under

Groupon has not been able to push its way into every international market. Whether they are clones of Groupon or had a similar group-buying idea earlier, many companies have resisted Andrew Mason's acquisition bids. In Australia, for instance, a company called Scoopon registered the Groupon.com.au domain name and filed for a trademark for the name Groupon. Scoopon refused a $300,000 offer from Mason to purchase the rights to both. Groupon sued, and the lawsuit remains unresolved. Meanwhile, Groupon operates in Australia under the name Stardeals.

In 2011, in preparation for New Year's Day celebrations, about five hundred customers of Groupon Japan—the former Qpod—used the company's services to buy discounted traditional holiday meals. They placed an order with Tokyo's Bird Café restaurant for *osechi*—very important, traditional meals that Japanese serve to celebrate the new year. Osechi are supposed to be beautifully presented and carefully prepared. But many of the meals arrived in terrible condition, and many more were delivered too late. Angry Japanese users lashed out online, and the mishap became a major embarrassment for the restaurant and for Groupon.

To make it up to them, Mason reimbursed all of the upset users who had paid the equivalent of $127 U.S. for each meal. He also gave them additional vouchers worth more than half that. He filmed and posted to YouTube a profuse apology, promising that it would not happen again. "We created Groupon to help enrich people's lives by bringing new, exciting experiences to them," he said, according to a report from the *Huffington Post*. "So when we do the opposite, as we have in this case, it really hurts."

Within a few weeks, however, Mason and Groupon would again find themselves rushing to control the damage done to their image both at home and abroad. This time, the audience was even bigger: the millions of viewers worldwide who tuned in for the year's biggest broadcasting event, the NFL Super Bowl. The commercials shown during the Super Bowl receive far more viewers—and buzz—than those broadcast at any other time of the year. Groupon hoped to make a big splash with an ad that it thought was quite clever.

In it, actor Timothy Hutton talks about Tibet in somber tones that make viewers anticipate a commercial for a human rights or humanitarian charitable organization: "Mountainous Tibet—one of the most beautiful places in the world. The people of Tibet are in trouble, their very culture in jeopardy...but they still whip up an amazing fish curry." In the end, the ad, far from highlighting the plight of Tibetans oppressed by an occupying and authoritarian Chinese regime, was merely publicizing a Groupon offer for a Tibetan eatery in Chicago.

The nation of Tibet has experienced great suffering during its occupation by neighboring China, and many viewers found the ad offensive. They thought it was tasteless to belittle the sometimes-violent history of the Chinese occupation to promote Groupon. They also attacked other, similar Groupon ads aired that night, which they felt also mocked other serious and meaningful causes. Others, however, defended Groupon, agreeing with Mason's explanation that it was a humorous way to spoof celebrities and their charity causes, while also poking fun

A photo still of Groupon's infamous Super Bowl ad, featuring actor Timothy Hutton discussing Tibetan cuisine. The ad, intended to be tongue-in-cheek, ignited a firestorm of controversy when it aired in early 2011.

at Groupon itself. Referring to one ad that mentioned the environmental organization Greenpeace, Mason insisted, "Not a single person watched our ad and concluded that it's cool to kill whales."

Links to the ads online also directed visitors to donate to genuine Tibetan and humanitarian organizations via Groupon's campaign, dubbed "Save the Money." Greenpeace even reported that Groupon had helped it raise money. The other organizations in the campaign defended the Super Bowl ads, saying they had raised public awareness of their mission and efforts. Mason saw the spoofy but still socially minded commercials and their online counterparts as perfectly natural and in harmony with Groupon's ethos. After all, Groupon had evolved from the socially conscious aims of the Point, yoking the potential of group action to a sense of fun, adventure, and pleasurable consumerism. In the end, however, Groupon bowed to the negative criticism and had the ads pulled.

In the wake of the Super Bowl brouhaha, many people thought Groupon had tripped up again. Mason issued a statement that defended Groupon's advertising decisions and expressed regret if anyone had taken offense or felt they were mocking noble and important causes. "We would never have run these ads if we thought they trivialized the causes," he wrote. "[E]ven if we didn't take them as seriously as we do, what type of company would go out of their way to be so antagonistic?"

THE CHALLENGE OF CHINA

Like many large international companies seeking to expand into large and untapped markets, Groupon had its eye on China early on. China had become an economic powerhouse in the first decade of the twenty-first century, and many Western companies recognized the opportunity to make a lot of money there, if they could only get a foothold.

The time seemed ripe for Groupon to enter China. The Chinese daily deals market was projected to grow ten times larger in 2011 than it was in 2010—from $300 million to $3 billion. There is also a longstanding culture of deals, discounts, and haggling (arguing with merchants over cheaper prices) in China. It seemed like a natural place for Groupon to succeed. Yet serious obstacles to its success in China loomed large.

One problem for many companies worldwide is the proliferation of Chinese-made imitations, or "knockoffs," of their products. These range from consumer goods like clothes, purses, CDs and DVDs, and electronics to intellectual property like business models and Web site ideas. Unlike other nations in which Groupon has set up shop, China already has not just dozens, but thousands, of startups very similar to the Groupon daily deal model.

China would be a challenge for Groupon to break into and flourish in, and not just because of the many clones in operation there. China's business and marketing culture can be very different from that of Western economies, or even other Asian ones such as Japan or Korea. In many industries, the Chinese business community and government regulations often heavily favor domestic, or home-grown, Chinese-owned-and-operated companies.

As a result of all these obstacles, it has taken longer for Groupon to set up operations in China's many middle-sized and large cities than it did for the company to become firmly established in North America, Europe, and other parts of Asia.

Groupon does have an ally within China, however: Tencent Holdings, the nation's second-largest Internet company. Tencent also runs the hugely popular QQ instant messaging platform and social network used by hundreds of millions of Chinese. Groupon initially hoped that QQ would give it immediate access to many of its users, but it has not been quite so simple.

FROM GROUPON TO GAOPENG.COM

Groupon was not alone in finding the Chinese market a tough nut to crack. Google had withdrawn part of its operation due to censorship issues. Other large companies like eBay and Yahoo! also had mixed results there.

One early roadblock for Groupon was that a Chinese competitor had already taken its company name. Unable to claim the name Groupon, Mason instead partnered with Tencent holdings to form GaoPeng. The name evokes a traditional Chinese idea about welcoming honored guests. Landing a name and partnership did not mark the end of Groupon/GaoPeng's struggles, however.

On the one hand, public opinion toward Groupon was mixed. Its Tibet-themed Super Bowl commercials (which ran just as the company was trying to break into Chinese markets), along with its pro-Tibet activism, were highly unpopular in China. Both the Chinese government and much of the public are highly sensitive about China's supposed right to Tibetan territory. Other observers pointed out that Groupon/GaoPeng was hiring too many foreigners (non-Chinese) in management and leadership positions. For a site that depends on appealing to users locally, this was widely seen as a big mistake.

More recently, GaoPeng/Groupon China has continued to face difficulties. While it is still the number one daily deal Web site in most of its markets worldwide, it is only number eight among Chinese firms. In August 2011, it was announced that ten offices throughout China had closed, with about four hundred employees laid off. According to Bloomberg News, Groupon said that it was still hiring and expanding in China, and that many of the laid-off employees had been let go for "poor performance."

In announcing the layoffs, GaoPeng's spokesperson said it planned to focus more on the middle- to large-sized cities in China where the daily deals market is more

Employees of Gaopeng.com, Groupon's daily deals venture in China, are shown at company offices in Shanghai, China. Groupon decided to downsize its efforts in China days earlier, sparking criticism that it failed to judge the intensely competitive Chinese market properly.

developed. The spokesperson insisted that Groupon "is fully committed to the Chinese market for the long term." Mason added, "China is definitely a different market, but every month we inch closer to profitability." Still, Groupon's

stumbles in China were not the best news to generate just ahead of a highly anticipated but increasingly uncertain IPO.

TOO BIG TOO SOON?

When it comes to growth, Web companies are often caught between a rock and a hard place. Growing too fast might overextend them. If they move too slowly, however, they run the risk of other companies stealing business from them and perhaps gaining dominance in the field. Thousands of Internet-based businesses have risen and fallen in the past two decades. Google, eBay, and Facebook are the success stories that people remember. Most of the others—especially the ones that fail to grow—are soon forgotten.

With imitators cloning its business model worldwide and increasingly fierce competition in the U.S. markets, Groupon needed to move fast. In the rush to conquer markets, however, any company, regardless of its product or service, risks compromising quality and making serious business mistakes. As Mason's company expanded, flaws began to appear in its business model, particularly when it came to merchant satisfaction with Groupon partnerships.

DISSATISFACTION AND
DISILLUSIONMENT WITH GROUPON

One problem for Groupon has been a curious one—sometimes its daily deals were *too* successful. In some cases, so many people sign up for a deal that a business, especially a small one, gets overwhelmed. A successful response to a Groupon coupon can be mixed: the deal puts the business on the map, but on a more immediate level, a business might not be able to honor the large number of deals that have been sold.

For instance, the *Chicago Tribune* reported on the Chicago Bagel Authority's negative experience with its Groupon partnership. It offered $3 Groupon vouchers for $8 worth of food items. After splitting the profits 50/50 with Groupon, however, the bagel shop made less than it had expected to. Plus, it had sold ten thousand Groupons, nearly ten times more than expected. This meant that the shop was forced to sell enormous quantities of food at a discount. Owner Gary Gibbs felt the whole idea was a mistake. He told the *Tribune*, "This will end up being the year of the Groupon for us, and that's not a good thing...We'll count it as a loss."

Common complaints from some restaurants that have partnered with Groupon have centered on people cashing in a coupon and then not tipping well or at all. Or some Groupon users would tip based on the discounted price of the meals, rather than the original price as they should. This became such an issue that Groupon began reminding users to tip generously for services. Business owners often take a dim view of Groupon coupon holders, regarding them as freeloaders who are unlikely to ever return without a coupon and pay full price for a good or service. Alternatively, Groupon users sometimes complain about bad service and rude treatment from impatient or contemptuous staff. They feel like they are treated as second-class citizens once they present their Groupon coupon.

Other businesses have had their phone lines overwhelmed by Groupon users. One hair salon that had partnered with Groupon was swamped with calls from coupon holders, preventing its regular customers from phoning in appointments. If a business does not prepare ahead of time for a potentially huge surge in customers, it can cause major headaches for owners, staff, and Groupon users.

Yet another problem is Groupon users taking unfair advantage of the deal and not rewarding the establishments with repeat business, loyalty, or even basic decency. David Yanda, co-owner of Chicago's Zapatista, a Mexican eatery, complained about this to the *Chicago Sun-Times*. While initially pleased with a sale of five thousand Groupons, Yanda said, "We didn't anticipate that we wouldn't make moncy or that the Groupon purchaser wouldn't come back to pay full price." Adding insult to injury, about 9 percent of the Groupon users who visited Zapatista had copied their one-time-only Groupons and used them as often as seven or eight times, said Yanda.

Some bloggers have publicized the weaknesses in the Groupon system, especially the copying or submitting of forged or doctored coupons. When one blog post showed the many ways one can reuse Groupon coupons, Mason responded, "[We've] accepted the fact that a business can never create enough rules to prevent bad people from taking advantage of them. So we just try to cultivate a community where everyone is cool to everyone else."

CHAPTER 6

Lessons Learned, Groupon Moves Forward

Groupon, faced with criticism, challenges, and bad news, continues to insist that its platform remains the world leader in daily deals. Responding to customer and merchant complaints, growth setbacks, and ever-growing competition is how it is working to remain on top. Andrew Mason remains as committed as ever to providing rewarding user and partner experiences. At the same time, it must look to the future and arm itself with the best possible strategies, technologies, partnerships, and personnel if it hopes to remain an industry leader.

KEEPING CUSTOMERS AND PARTNERS HAPPY

Groupon's sales teams have learned from their missteps and setbacks. Their solutions include helping businesses better prepare for a crush of visitors following the issuing of a Groupon deal. If a daily deal causes an eatery to force its customers to wait too long for a table, it is a bad experience for both the business and the customers. The same is true if a business must rush to prepare a product or service of lesser quality in order to meet a sudden spike in Groupon-driven customer demand.

Andrew Mason has declared that the happiness of merchants and customers is always a top priority for Groupon and its staff. This extends to the company's flexible return policy. In July 2010, Mason told Mixergy.com, "If anyone ever feels like Groupon let them down after having used a Groupon, we'll give a refund, no questions asked." This is known within and outside the company as the "Groupon Promise," and it extends even to those who have not redeemed their deal.

Another unique feature is the company's twenty-four-hour-a-day hotline. Mason and Groupon feel it's extremely important that customers can reach a live human being on the phone at any time to respond to any mistakes or problems that they experience.

The company also says it takes complaints from merchants about profit sharing very seriously. One change that Groupon has made is adjusting, in some cases, its normal 50/50 profit share arrangement with merchants. For those businesses that feel it does not make sense to try Groupon because there is too little to gain, earning a larger percentage of each offer's profit sweetens the deal. Some local merchants are signing deals in which

A Groupon user enjoys a half-price meal at Galletto Ristorante in Modesto, California. Despite some stumbles, Andrew Mason and Groupon hope to continue their company's explosive growth while satisfying users, merchant partners, investors, and shareholders.

Groupon receives 35 to 45 percent of the cut, instead of the traditional 50 percent. National merchants are even negotiating arrangements in which Groupon only takes 5 to 25 percent of the profit.

Mason's philosophy is to always be on the offensive. He believes concentrating on customer service and generating new business will keep Groupon competitive and creative. It will make Groupon proactive, rather than merely reactive to competition. As he told *Vanity Fair* in August 2011, Groupon will slip up only if it repeats the mistakes of other companies and "start[s] doing things that are designed for the purpose of crushing competition instead of things that are designed to make their customers happy."

THE CALM BEFORE THE STORM: GETTING READY FOR A GROUPON

It is simply the nature of the business that not all merchants will have an ideal experience partnering with Groupon. Mason tries to minimize the chances of a disappointing experience by giving merchants a breakdown of exactly what to expect. He also offers advice on how to deal effectively and profitably with the sudden influx of business following the release of a Groupon daily deal. One solution for a small business is to expand capacity in preparation for its Groupon offer. A restaurant may want to add more seats, extend its hours, or hire more employees to accommodate the increase in volume.

Another step has been to beef up the portion of Groupon's staff that is dedicated to working with merchants, as company spokeswoman Julie Mossler told the *Chicago Tribune* in August 2011. "We certainly believe in learning from past experiences," she said. Using a health spa as an example, she elaborated, "If you [the spa] know you can't handle this level of traffic, either you need to staff up…open your books and allow more appointments, or we can put you in a personalized deal or put in a cap." Capping, or limiting, the amount of coupons sold is one way that Groupon works with merchants to make sure that they don't overextend themselves.

DEFENDING GROUPON

Though Mason has worked hard to address merchant complaints, many observers feel that business owners are failing to appreciate the boost that Groupon gives them. Eric Lefkofsky told the *Sun-Times*, "If people cannot manage the flow of customers, they may not be happy. It's easy to blame Groupon or someone else. [However] as an ad vehicle to get new customers, it is adding huge value."

Mason himself has also fiercely defended Groupon and questioned what he views as unfair media criticism. In a memo to employees in late August 2011, he pointed out that Groupon remained the leader in the daily deals industry and that the size of its business was something that its competitors could not match. He observed that the "real point is that our business is a lot harder to build than people realize, and our scale creates competitive advantages that even the largest technology companies are having trouble penetrating." Mason added that U.S. revenue for August 2011 would jump 12 percent from the previous month, while marketing expenses would fall by 20 percent. In its IPO filings in June 2011, Groupon reported that it had eighty-three million subscribers in forty-three nations, with almost fifty-seven thousand local merchants participating.

GROUPON'S ROAD AHEAD: INNOVATIONS

What will Groupon do next? Following its highly publicized IPO and new status as a publicly-traded company, it remains to be seen where Mason will take the company in the future. Groupon's business model is incredibly easy to copy. So the challenge for Mason and his team is to maintain the human element that they cherish, but also develop and use new technology to create experiences for users that competitors have not thought of yet.

TAILORED DEALS

It is likely that new services that are more tailored to individual users and their needs and preferences could be the key to the future of the daily deals market. Groupon CFO Jason Child told AOL's DailyFinance in February 2011: "We're going to continue to expand the model beyond the deal of the day.

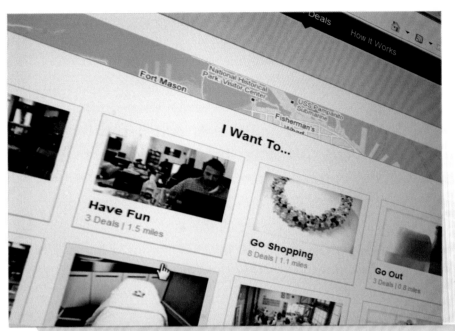

This Groupon screenshot demonstrates the company's desire to position itself as the go-to marketplace for almost any conceivable activity. Groupon's future will surely depend on making such choices available on all platforms, including smartphones and tablets.

It could be deal of the day or deal of the hour or even 'What do you want to do today?' There are a lot of directions to go."

In August 2010, Groupon began to experiment with personalized deals, testing these services in Chicago and other cities. These deals were tailored to users' gender, neighborhood, income, and other demographic factors. Eventually, this personal touch could allow Groupon to offer more than one deal per day. On top of that, it will probably deliver these offers via any current or future mobile platform (for example, via smartphones, tablets, and other mobile devices).

Groupon Stores

An already-existing Groupon service is Groupon Stores, which is basically a virtual online storefront in which Groupon merchants can display deals. These offers differ from the Groupon daily deal in that they can be as frequent and numerous as the merchant likes. Groupon tells merchants that opening a Groupon Store online—accessible via the main Groupon site—can take as little as a few minutes. Merchants control the terms of the deals and offer them to those customers who frequent their businesses online, including anyone who has once used a Groupon for their goods and services in the past. Groupon takes a small commission on each deal, while the merchant keeps the rest of the profit.

GROUPON NOW!

Another innovation for Groupon has been the introduction of Groupon Now! to several North American cities in 2011. Expanding on the daily deal idea, the service, with its own application available for smartphones and other mobile devices, lets businesses offer deals in real time. Rather than sell hundreds of Groupon coupons and then worry about being able to handle all those

Groupon Now! was launched by the company in order to attract users to highly customized, hyper-local deals in real time, based on a user's specific location and preferences.

new customers, a merchant can pick and choose when it makes deals available. Say a local restaurant had a busy lunch hour but is nearly empty come dinnertime. A few well-targeted Groupons can attract a rush of customers within an hour or two and fill tables during a traditionally slow period of the day.

Groupon Now! provides users with lists of active deals only a short distance away. A pop-up screen titled "I want to..." comes up, with a range of possible activities and services. Users can choose from several options, including "Go out," "Go shopping," "Visit a museum," and more. It also tells how many deals under each category are available and how far away they are. For instance, if a person wanted to eat something, he or she might discover twenty possible deals only a few blocks away.

The merchants have the freedom to pick what they want to sell, when they want to sell it and for how long (it can be as short as a one- or two-hour window of opportunity if desired), and at what level of discount. The real-time offers generally don't include the requirement that the deal "tips"—that a certain number of people must sign up for it to be activated. Instead the emphasis is on getting customers in immediately.

Mason sees this real-time connectivity as the next logical step in how millions will be shopping worldwide soon. Tying together real-time alerts to the specific shopping habits and preferences of particular users is an important goal for the future.

"CHECKING IN" WITH GROUPON

In July 2011, Groupon signed a deal with Foursquare, the popular location-based service (LBS). Foursquare lets users find each other, "check in" to locations in real time, and occasionally receive discounts or prizes from merchants whose businesses are Foursquare locations.

Foursquare users in the United States and Canada now have access to Groupon deals, including Groupon Now!, which appear as an option on Foursquare's Explore tab. Foursquare users can also redeem special, instantaneous deals when they check in to a restaurant or other place of business.

The addition of both Groupon Now! and Foursquare applications helps address two of the lingering complaints against Groupon: that deals are inconvenient for users to cash in and are a major headache for suddenly swamped businesses.

Slate.com writer Noreen Malone experimented with using Groupon deals for a whole week as her sole method of spending. She discovered that traveling to redeem deals was sometimes difficult. She wrote, "It's rare that they [Groupons] are truly geographically convenient— one reason why so many go unused." A half-off deal for a restaurant that might require two hours of round-trip travel might never get used.

Sometimes Groupons are inconvenient because of time restrictions. People get excited and sign up for a deal, but never end up using it because the offer expires before they get around to using the coupon. With real-time apps, people could arrange to be offered deals for only specific things (meals, massages, etc.) at particular times, when they really have the time and inclination.

Another benefit of zeroing in ever more closely on customer preferences and habits is being able to manage deals more efficiently. With sales teams being able to direct people in a smaller area to local businesses, the old problem of overselling deals to overwhelmed businesses will decrease. Also, if specific deals are limited to nearby users, there is a greater likelihood that local consumers will become repeat customers.

GROUPON LOOKS TO THE FUTURE

The ups and downs of running and growing a company worth billions of dollars keep Andrew Mason sharp and realistic. He stresses the importance of taking chances and being ready for setbacks, even big ones. "Being on the lookout for failure is essential for me to run the business. You have to remind yourself to be afraid," he told *Time Out Chicago* in December 2011.

Part of his personal strategy is to always stay humble and not evolve into what he sees as a "typical" CEO. To ensure that he "keeps it real," he periodically visits his mentor and former boss Steve Albini. Mason told *Time Out Chicago*, "I like to see him every few months so I can make sure I'm still the same person."

The same may be said of Groupon, and its challenge is related to Mason's: Can it stay vital and popular, and deliver what it always has without losing its way?

Only time will tell. Like many of the Web-based companies whose successes it hopes to replicate, Groupon has been a game-changer. Whatever the future holds, it has certainly made its mark on how and where people shop, make purchasing decisions, spend their time, and experience their neighborhoods. It has revolutionized the ways in which we interact with our local economy, including our neighborhood businesses and merchants. On a very real level, Groupon has changed the way we live and experience the world around us. For this reason, there is a good chance that the daily deal company—and Andrew Mason—will continue to surprise us and prove the critics wrong.

Fact Sheet on

ANDREW MASON

Birthdate: 1981 (Exact date unrevealed)

Birthplace: Mt. Lebanon, Pennsylvania

Current residence: Chicago, Illinois

Colleges attended: Northwestern University, 1999–2003; University of Chicago/Harris School of Public Policy (2006; dropped out three months into master's program)

Estimated net worth: $700 million to over $1 billion (depending on fluctuations in Groupon stock prices)

First important entrepreneurial effort: Bagel Express (wholesale bagels resold to neighbors at market value plus service and delivery fee)

Important mentors: Steve Albini, Eric Lefkofsky

Important software developed: Policy Tree

Former company: ThePoint.com

Fact Sheet on
GROUPON INC.

Date formed: October 2008 (as a subsidiary service of the Point)

Official launch: November 2008

First daily deal: Two-for-one pizzas at Motel Bar, Chicago, Illinois

Date of IPO: November 3, 2011

Annual revenue: Undetermined

Net worth: $12.8 billion (on day of IPO)

Current assets (June 1, 2011 SEC documents): $225 million

Estimated debts (June 1, 2011 SEC documents): $392 million

Number of users: Approximately 115 million (as of September 2011)

Number of employees: 9,625 (as of June 30, 2011)

Headquarters: Chicago, Illinois

Revenue, 2nd quarter 2011: $878,018,000

Number of nations Groupon operates in: 45

Number of cities Groupon operates in: 565

Timeline

1981 Andrew Mason is born in Mt. Lebanon, Pennsylvania.

2003 Mason graduates from Northwestern University and goes to work as a software designer for Chicago entrepreneur Eric Lefkofsky at InnerWorkings, a print procurement services company.

2006 Mason enrolls in the University of Chicago's Harris School of Public Policy but drops out of the master's program after three months; interns with famed recording engineer Steve Albini at Electrical Audio; develops the Policy Tree Web site.

2007 Mason's Web site the Point is officially launched.

October 2008 Groupon starts as a subsidiary service of the Point.

November 2008 Groupon offers its first daily deal.

March 2009 Groupon offers its first Boston deal in its first major expansion.

May 2009 Groupon launches operations in New York City.

August 2009 Groupon expands into Atlanta, Dallas, Los Angeles, San Diego, and Seattle.

April 2010 Groupon raises $135 million from Russian investment firm Digital Sky Technologies.

May 2010 Groupon acquires CityDeal, the German-based daily deals Web site that is the leader in the European market.

August 2010 Groupon purchases Darberry and Qpod, the Russian and Japanese daily deals companies; has its largest daily deal, a national discount offer with retail giant the Gap; sells its ten-millionth Groupon.

January 2011 Groupon announces it has raised $950 million in venture capital.

February 2011 Groupon airs a controversial ad campaign during the Super Bowl that seems to mock the cause of Tibetan independence, raising a storm of criticism.

June 2011 Groupon files paperwork for an initial public offering (IPO).

August 2011 Groupon revises its controversial ACSOI figures, giving investors and financial analysts a more realistic, but now far less positive, snapshot of its finances.

September 2011 Due to an unpredictable stock market and worldwide economic uncertainty, Groupon postpones its IPO indefinitely.

November 2011 Groupon goes public, selling 35 million shares at $20 each, for a total valuation of $12.8 billion. Three weeks later, Groupon stocks plummet to as low as $14 per share from a high of $31.

Glossary

adjusted consolidated segment operating income (ACSOI) A controversial accounting tactic in which the reporting of certain expenses is spread out over a period of time.

chief financial officer (CFO) The person in a corporation who manages financial risks for the organization and is often in charge of financial record keeping and related tasks.

clone A company, product, or service that very closely imitates another.

copy Written content, usually composed for marketing or advertising purposes.

corporate culture The collective set of traditions, values, and rules that members of an organization apply to their actions within that organization and to their actions taken in an official capacity when interacting with the world outside.

culture shock The difficulty that people (and businesses) face when trying to adjust, adapt to, and thrive in a nation, society, or culture very different from their own.

daily deal The business model pioneered by Groupon in which users are offered significant discounts on goods and services in a daily, Internet-delivered promotion.

demographics The study of characteristics of populations—such as age, income, location, and ethnicity—that helps businesses market their services to customers.

dot-com A company whose business is mostly or entirely Internet-based.

dot-com bubble An era of great investment and growth in Web-based businesses, made possible by the enormous popularity of the Internet, lasting from about 1995 to 2000.

e-commerce The buying and selling of products and services online.

entrepreneur A person who starts a business.

Foursquare One of the most popular location-based services.

hyper-local Describing services that cater to a very limited, or local, area or community.

improv Theater or comedy created spontaneously on stage by unscripted performers.

initial public offering (IPO) The initial sale of stock by a previously private company to the general public.

irreverent Lacking the expected or proper respect or seriousness in a situation.

location-based service (LBS) A mobile platform, often enabled with a social media component, that tracks users' movements in real-time to allow them to exchange information, especially about their environment as they explore it.

osechi Traditional, elaborate meals enjoyed by Japanese households during New Year celebrations.

overhead The standard costs that companies must take into account to run their business, including rent, salaries, supplies, and research and development.

petition A letter that people sign in support of the letter's message and that is ultimately delivered to a person, company, or government official in the hopes of effecting a desired course of action or change in policy.

pitch A planned presentation by a seller to get someone to purchase a good or service.

public company A company that trades its ownership shares on the stock market and must make a profit for its shareholders, or collective owners.

quarter A three-month period of economic activity.

recession An economic downturn in the business cycle, usually defined as six months or more of declining growth in the economy.

reimburse To pay someone for an expense that he or she has incurred; a company may reimburse customers for money they spent on a product or service that they were unhappy with.

Securities and Exchange Commission (SEC) The federal agency that regulates the securities industry. All public companies must adhere to SEC rules.

social media A wide range of Web- and mobile-based technological platforms, including Web sites, in which users socialize by exchanging user-created content. Examples are Facebook and Twitter.

start-up A new technology-based company, often a dot-com, that is perceived to have great economic potential.

tipping point In terms of Groupon, the point at which enough users sign on to a deal to activate it.

venture capital Money invested in a promising young company by other companies or entities; investment firms that specialize in this are known as venture capital firms.

voucher A type of document that gives the owner or user a particular monetary value to exchange for goods or services.

Web 2.0 The name for the newest generation of Internet applications and sites that arose in the 2000s, usually emphasizing social media elements such as user-generated content, collaboration, and applications that are interoperable, or can work easily with each other.

For More Information

Association of Internet Researchers (AOIR)
910 West Van Buren Street, #142
Chicago, IL 60607
Web site: http://aoir.org
An academic association dedicated to studying various
aspects of the Internet, the AOIR sponsors research
and holds conferences worldwide.

Berkley Center for Entrepreneurship & Innovation
New York University/Stern School of Business
Henry Kaufman Management Center, Suite 7-150
44 West 4th Street
New York, NY 10012
(212) 998-0070
Web site: http://www.stern.nyu.edu/experience-stern/
about/departments-centers-initiatives/centers-of-
research/berkley-center/center-overview/index.htm
The Berkley Center at NYU/Stern is dedicated to helping students become entrepreneurs in a wide variety
of fields.

Bureau of Consumer Protection: Computers and
the Internet
Federal Trade Commission (FTC)
600 Pennsylvania Avenue NW
Washington, DC 20580
(202) 326-2222
Web site: http://www.ftc.gov
The FTC's Bureau of Consumer Protection provides
resources and contact information to answer questions or complaints about online business.

Canada Business
151 Yonge Street, 3rd floor
Toronto, ON M5C 2W7
Canada
(888) 745-8888
Web site: http://www.canadabusiness.ca
Canada Business is a federal service of the Canadian government dedicated to helping foster entrepreneurship
and innovation by providing resources to new and
existing business owners.

Center for Research in Electronic Commerce
McCombs School of Business
University of Texas at Austin
1 University Station, B6000

Austin, TX 78712-1178

(512) 471-5921

Web site: http://cism.mccombs.utexas.edu

The University of Texas at Austin's McCombs School of Business is a leading center of academic studies dealing in e-commerce.

Chicagoland Entrepreneurial Center (CEC)

Aon Center

200 East Randolph Street, Suite 2200

Chicago, IL 60601-6436

Web site: http://www.chicagolandec.org

The Chicagoland Entrepreneurial Center helps promote and grow start-ups in Andrew Mason's hometown of Chicago.

Department of Entrepreneurship

Ted Rogers School of Management

Ryerson University

350 Victoria Street

Toronto, ON M5B 2K3

Canada

Web site: http://www.ryerson.ca

Ryerson, one of Canada's top universities, offers an intensive program for entrepreneurs hoping to make it big.

Institute for Technology Entrepreneurship &
    Commercialization
Boston University School of Management
595 Commonwealth Avenue
Boston, MA 02215
(617) 353-9391
Web site: http://www.bu.edu/itec
Boston University's Technology Entrepreneurship &
    Commercialization program is dedicated to giving
    valuable training to undergraduate and gradu-
    ate students hoping to innovate in the "knowledge
    economy."

National Venture Capital Association (NVCA)
1655 North Fort Myer Drive, Suite 850
Arlington, VA 22209
(703) 524-2549
Web site: http://www.nvca.org
The NVCA is the main trade association for venture
    capitalists in the United States, with a stated mis-
    sion of promoting innovation through investment.

U.S. Securities and Exchange Commission (SEC)
100 F Street NE
Washington, DC 20549
(202) 942-8088

Web site: http://www.sec.gov
The SEC is the federal agency that regulates the activities
of public companies.

Women in Ecommerce
P.O. Box 550856
Fort Lauderdale, FL 33355-0856
(954) 625-6606
Web site: http://www.wecai.org
Women in Ecommerce is a business association and
social networking community helping promote suc-
cess for women working in Web-based business.

WEB SITES

Due to the changing nature of Internet links, Rosen Publishing has developed an online list of Web sites related
to the subject of this book. This site is updated regularly.
Please use this link to access the list:

http://www.rosenlinks.com/ibio/mason

For Further Reading

Duffield, Katy. *Chad Hurley, Steve Chen, Jawed Karim: YouTube Creators* (Innovators). Farmington Hills, MI: KidHaven, 2008.

Freese, Susan M. *Craigslist: The Company and Its Founder* (Technology Pioneers). Edina, MN: Essential Library, 2011.

Gilbert, Sara. *The Story of eBay* (Built for Success). Mankato, MN: Creative Paperbacks, 2011.

Gilbert, Sara. *The Story of Google* (Built for Success). Mankato, MN: Creative Paperbacks, 2011.

Gitlin, Martin. *Ebay: The Company and Its Founder* (Technology Pioneers). Edina, MN: Essential Library, 2011.

Hamen, Susan E. *Google: The Company and Its Founders* (Technology Pioneers). Edina, MN: Essential Library, 2011.

Hasday, Judy L. *Facebook and Mark Zuckerberg* (Business Leaders). Greensboro, NC: Morgan Reynolds Publishing, 2011.

Jones, Bradley L. *Web 2.0 Heroes: Interviews with 20 Web 2.0 Influencers*. Hoboken, NJ: Wiley, 2008.

Kirkpatrick, David. *The Facebook Effect: The Inside Story of the Company That Is Connecting the World.* New York, NY: Simon & Schuster, 2011.

Lewis, Michael F. *Social Media Leadership: How to Get Off the Bench and Into the Game.* Atlanta, GA: Leigh Walker Books, 2011.

Lowe, Janet. *Google Speaks: Secrets of the World's Greatest Billionaire Entrepreneurs, Sergey Brin and Larry Page.* Hoboken, NJ: Wiley, 2009.

Lusted, Marcia Amidon. *Social Networking: MySpace, Facebook, and Twitter* (Technology Pioneers). Edina, MN: Essential Library, 2011.

McPherson, Stephanie Sammartino. *Sergey Brin and Larry Page: Founders of Google* (USA Today Lifeline Biographies). Breckenridge, CO: Twenty-First Century Books, 2010.

Meyer, Marc H. *Entrepreneurship: An Innovator's Guide to Start-ups and Corporate Ventures.* Thousand Oaks, CA: Sage Publications, 2010.

Meyerson, Mitch, ed. *Success Secrets of Social Media Marketing Superstars.* Irvine, CA: Entrepreneur Press, 2010.

Musolf, Nell. *The Story of Microsoft* (Built for Success). Mankato, MN: Creative Paperbacks, 2011.

Robinson, Tom. *Jeff Bezos: Amazon.com Architect* (Publishing Pioneers). Edina, MN: ABDO Publishing, 2009.

Safko, Lon. *The Social Media Bible: Tactics, Tools, and Strategies for Business Success*. Hoboken, NJ: Wiley, 2010.

Stewart, Gail B. *Mark Zuckerberg, Facebook Creator (Innovators)*. Farmington Hills, MI: KidHaven, 2009.

Tang, Stanley. *eMillions: Behind-the-Scenes Stories of 14 Successful Internet Millionaires*. New York, NY: Morgan James Publishing, 2008.

Walsh, Bob. *The Web Start-up Success Guide* (Books for Professionals by Professionals). New York, NY: Apress, 2008.

Willis, Laurie. *Web 2.0* (Social Issues Firsthand). Farmington Hills, MI: Greenhaven Press, 2009.

Bibliography

Aaker, Jennifer, and Andy Smith. *The Dragonfly Effect: Quick, Effective, and Powerful Ways to Use Social Media to Drive Social Change.* San Francisco, CA: Jossey-Bass, 2010.

Albanesius, Chloe. "Groupon Talks Privacy, Always-on Location Tracking." *PC Magazine*, August 19, 2011. Retrieved August 2011 (http://www.pcmag.com/article2/0,2817,2391391,00.asp).

Austin, Scott. "Groupon's Super Bowl Ad Quickly Draws Backlash." *Wall Street Journal*, February 6, 2011. Retrieved July 2011 (http://blogs.wsj.com/venturecapital/2011/02/06/that-was-fast-groupons-super-bowl-ad-draws-backlash-video).

Austin, Scott. "Will Investors Take Groupon's Andrew Mason Seriously?" *Wall Street Journal*, June 7, 2011. Retrieved July 2011 (http://blogs.wsj.com/venturecapital/2011/06/07/will-investors-take-groupons-andrew-mason-seriously).

Bishop, Bill. "Groupon China Is a Disaster—Will the Company Just Give Up?" Business Insider, August 24, 2011. Retrieved August 2011 (http://www.businessinsider.com/will-groupon-china-expire-2011-8).

Bishop, Bill. "Is Tencent the Wrong Partner for Groupon in China?" Digicha.com, August 8, 2011. Retrieved

August 2011 (http://digicha.com/index.php/2011/08/
is-tencent-the-wrong-partner-for-groupon-in-china).

Bishop, Bill. "Will Groupon China Expire?" Digicha.
com, August 24, 2011. Retrieved August 2011 (http://
digicha.com/index.php/2011/08/will-groupon-
china-expire).

Booton, Jennifer. "Groupon Snags Another Google
Executive." FOX Business, April 22, 2011. Retrieved
July 2011 (http://www.foxbusiness.com/
technology/2011/04/22/groupon-poaches-
google-executive).

Briggs, Bill. "Quirky CEO 'Genius' Behind Groupon's
Success." MSNBC, December 12, 2010.
Retrieved July 2011 (http://www.msnbc.msn.
com/id/40494597/ns/business-us_business/t/
quirky-ceo-genius-behind-groupons-success).

Brockman, John, ed. *Is the Internet Changing the Way You
Think?: The Net's Impact on Our Minds and Future.*
New York, NY: Harper Perennial, 2011

Burkeman, Oliver. "Groupon: The Golden Nugget."
Guardian, June 11, 2011. Retrieved August 2011
(http://www.guardian.co.uk/technology/2011/jun/
11/groupon-internet-andrew-mason-interview).

Carney, John. "Can Groupon Really Reduce Its Marketing
Costs?" CNBC, June 3, 2011. Retrieved August 2011
(http://www.cnbc.com/id/43271912/Can_Groupon_
Really_Reduce_Its_Marketing_Costs).

Carr, Nicholas. *The Big Switch: Rewiring the World, from Edison to Google*. New York, NY: W. W. Norton & Co., 2009.

Chan, Edwin. "Groupon's CEO Lashes Out at Critics Ahead of IPO." Reuters, August 26, 2011. Retrieved August 2011 (http://www.reuters.com/article/2011/08/26/groupon-ipo-idUSN1E77O22B 20110826).

Channick, Robert, and Wailin Wong. "Growing with Groupon May Be Tricky for Businesses." *Chicago Tribune*, August 16, 2010. Retricved August 2011 (http://articles.chicagotribune.com/2010-08-16/business/ct-biz-0816-groupon-20100816_1_groupon-businesses-chairs).

Chao, Loretta. "Groupon Stumbles in China, Closes Some Offices." *Wall Street Journal*, August 24, 2011. Retrieved August 2011 (http://online.wsj.com/article/SB1000142 4053111904279004576526283328853022.html).

Coburn, Lawrence. "Groupon CEO Andrew Mason Talks Growth, Clones, and Why Groupon Isn't a Coupon Site." The Next Web, March 24, 2010. Retrieved July 2011 (http://thenextweb.com/location/2010/03/24/groupon-ceo-andrew-mason-talks-growth-clones-groupon-coupon-site).

Coburn, Marcia Froelke. "On Groupon and Its Founder, Andrew Mason." *Chicago*, August 2010. Retrieved July 2011 (http://www.chicagomag.com/

Chicago-Magazine/August-2010/On-Groupon-and-its-founder-Andrew-Mason).

Collins, Hugh. "Groupon CFO Jason Child: 'I Don't See Any Limits.'" Daily Finance/AOL, February 8, 2011. Retrieved July 2011 (http://www.dailyfinance.com/2011/02/08/groupon-cfo-jason-child-i-dont-see-any-limits).

Comm, Joel. *Click Here to Order: Stories of the World's Most Successful Internet Marketing Entrepreneurs.* New York, NY: Morgan James Publishing, 2008.

De La Merced, Michael J. "Groupon Chief to Make $575 in 2011." *New York Times*, June 2, 2011. Retrieved August 2011 (http://dealbook.nytimes.com/2011/06/02/groupon-c-e-o-to-make-575-in-2011).

DeNinno, Nadine. "Top 12 Daily Deal Groupon Copycat Discount Web Sites." *International Business Times*, August 31, 2011. Retrieved September 2011 (http://www.ibtimes.com/articles/206670/20110831/top-12-best-daily-deal-groupon-copycat-discount-web-sites.htm).

Dholakia, Utpal M. "How Businesses Fare with Daily Deals: A Multi-Site Analysis of Groupon, LivingSocial, OpenTable, Travelzoo, and BuyWithMe Promotions." Rice University/Jones Graduate School of Business, June 13, 2011. Retrieved August 2011 (http://fortunebrainstormtech.files.wordpress.com/2011/06/ssrn-id1863466.pdf).

Dries, Kate. "At Groupon, Employees Don't Sell
Out, They Sell In." WBEZ Radio, May 31, 2011.
Retrieved July 2011 (http://www.wbez.org/story/
groupon-employees-dont-sell-out-they-sell-87240).

Duryee, Tricia. "Groupon Brings Group-Buying Concept
to Concert-Goers with Ticketmaster Partnership." All
Things D/Wall Street Journal Digital, May 9, 2011.
Retrieved July 2011 (http://allthingsd.com/20110509/
groupon-brings-group-buying-concept-to-concert-
goers-with-ticketmaster-partnership).

Etter, Lauren. "Groupon Therapy." *Vanity Fair*, August
2011. Retrieved August 2011 (http://www.vanityfair.
com/business/features/2011/08/groupon-201108).

Fast Company. "50 Most Innovative Companies: #5,
Groupon: For Reinvigorating Retail—and Turning
Down $6 Billion." February 2011. Retrieved August
2011 (http://www.fastcompany.com/most-innovative-
companies/2011/profile/groupon.php).

Finkle, Jim. "Groupon Files to Raise Up to $950 Million."
Reuters, December 29, 2010. Retrieved July 2011
(http://www.reuters.com/article/2010/12/29/us-
groupon-idUSTRE6BR3XD20101229).

Frommer, Dan. "Tour Groupon, The Funniest Start-up
We've Ever Been To." Business Insider, November 23,
2010. Retrieved July 2011 (http://www.businessinsider.
com/groupon-office-tour-2010-11).

Gustin, Sam. "Groupon IPO Could Value Company at Over $15 Billion." Wired.com, June 2, 2011. Retrieved July 2011 (http://www.wired.com/epicenter/2011/06/groupon-ipo).

Guy, Sandra. "Groupon Offers Refunds After Complaints About Flower Deal." *Chicago Sun-Times*, February 17, 2011. Retrieved July 2011 (http://www.suntimes.com/business/3822291-420/more-groupon-woes.html).

Haas, Benjamin. "Groupon Enters a Crowded Market for Deals in China." *Chicago Tribune*, May 9, 2011. Retrieved September 2011 (http://articles.chicagotribune.com/2011-05-09/business/ct-biz-0509-china-groupon-20110509_1_daily-deal-sites-groupon-chinese-operations).

Hickins, Michael. "Groupon Revenue Hit $760 Million, CEO Memo Shows." *Wall Street Journal*, February 26, 2011. Retrieved July 2011 (http://online.wsj.com/article/SB1000142405274870340860457164641411042376.html?mod=e2tw).

Hosaka, Tomoko A. "Groupon CEO Apologies to Japanese Customers." *Huffington Post*, January 17, 2011. Retrieved August 2011 (http://www.huffingtonpost.com/2011/01/17/groupon-ceo-apologizes-to_n_809894.html).

International Business Times. "LivingSocial vs. Groupon: Which One to Use." June 29, 2011.

Retrieved August 2011 (http://www.ibtimes.com/articles/171567/20110629/groupon-livingsocial-daily-deals.htm).

Jackson, Nicholas. "The Fall of Groupon: Is the Daily Deals Site Running Out of Cash?" *Atlantic*, August 19, 2011. Retrieved September 2011 (http://www.theatlantic.com/technology/archive/2011/08/the-fall-of-groupon-is-the-daily-deals-site-running-out-of-cash/243863).

Kallen, Stuart A. *The Information Revolution*. San Diego, CA: Lucent Books, 2010.

Kelleher, Kevin. "Does Mason Want to Get Out of Groupon?" *Fortune*/CNN, June 6, 2011. Retricved July 2011 (http://tech.fortune.cnn.com/2011/06/06/does-mason-want-to-get-out-of-groupon).

Kessler, Sarah. "LivingSocial Says It Will Overtake Groupon in January." Mashable.com, March 24, 2011. Retrieved July 2011 (http://mashable.com/2011/03/24/livingsocial-says-it-will-overtake-groupon-in-january-2012).

Krisher, Tom. "Groupon Users Furious About FTD Flower Deal." *Huffington Post*, February 13, 2011. Retrieved July 2011 (http://www.huffingtonpost.com/2011/02/13/groupon-ftd-deal_n_822360.html).

Kruger, Jennifer. "Groupon Now! Enters Four More North American Markets." PMA Newsline, June 17, 2011. Retrieved July 2011 (http://pmanewsline.

com/2011/06/17/groupon-now-enter-four-more-north-american-markets).

Lee, Thomas. "Dinner Is on Eric Lefkofsky: Groupon Co-Founder and U-M Alum Pockets $300M+ from Stock Sales, More to Come from IPO." Xconomy. com, June 3, 2011. Retrieved July 2011 (http://www. xconomy.com/detroit/2011/06/03/dinner-is-on-eric-lefkofsky-groupon-co-founder-and-u-m-alum-pockets-300m-from-stock-sales-more-to-come-from-ipo).

Lefkofsky, Eric. *Accelerated Disruption: Understanding the True Speed of Innovation.* Westport, CT: Easton Studio Press, 2007.

Levy, Steven. *Hackers: Heroes of the Computer Revolution—25th Anniversary Edition.* Sebastopol, CA: O'Reilly Media, 2010.

Lowrey, Annie. "Are Groupon's Creative Performance Metrics Masking Problems with Its Business?" Slate. com, August 11, 2011. Retrieved August 2011 (http:// www.slate.com/id/2301408).

MacMillan, Douglas. "Groupon's Venture in China Is Said to Fire Employees for Poor Performance." Bloomberg News, August 23, 2011. Retrieved August 2011 (http://www.bloomberg.com/news/2011-08-23/ groupon-china-joint-venture-said-to-fire-workers-for-poor-performance.html).

MacMillan, Douglas, and Lee Spears. "Groupon Reports Quarterly Loss After Abandoning Controversial

Accounting." Bloomberg News, August 10, 2011. Retrieved August 2011 (http://www.bloomberg.com/news/2011-07-29/groupon-s-digestive-problems-at-sec-may-delay-ipo-former-official-says.html).

Malone, Noreen. "My Groupon Week: What I Learned by Living Off Internet Coupons for Seven Straight Days." Slate.com, June 28, 2011. Retrieved July 2011 (http://www.slate.com/id/2297775).

McBride, Sarah. "Competition and Humor Drive Groupon's Andrew Mason." Reuters, June 3, 2011. Retrieved July 2011 (http://www.reuters.com/article/2011/06/03/us-groupon-idUSTRE7526TX20110603).

Mitchell, Dan. "Study Offers Grim News on Deal Sites Like Groupon." CNN Money, June 16, 2011. Retrieved July 2011 (http://tech.fortune.cnn.com/2011/06/16/study-offers-grim-news-on-daily-deals).

Mixergy. "The Story of Groupon: From Failure to an Industry-Changing, Profit Machine—with Andrew Mason." July 5, 2010. Retrieved August 2011 (http://mixergy.com/andrew-mason-groupon-interview).

Netter, Sarah. "Groupon Founder Andrew Mason 'Just Wanted to Work on Cool Stuff.'" ABC News, December 9, 2010. Retrieved July 2011 (http://abcnews.go.com/Business/groupon-founder-andrew-mason-wanted-work-cool-stuff/story?id=12348325).

Ostrow, Adam. "Groupon Files for $750 Million IPO." Mashable.com, June 2, 2011. Retrieved August 2011 (http://mashable.com/2011/06/02/groupon-ipo).

Ovide, Shira. "Groupon IPO: It's Here!" *Wall Street Journal*, June 2, 2011. Retrieved August 2011 (http://blogs.wsj.com/deals/2011/06/02/groupon-ipo-its-here).

Patel, Kunar. "Can Consumers Forgive Groupon's Ad Gaffe?" *Advertising Age*, February 14, 2011. Retrieved July 2011 (http://adage.com/article/news/consumers-forgive-groupon-s-super-bowl-ad-gaffe/148860).

Pletz, John. "Behind Dazzling Growth Story, Groupon Struggles to Keep Customers Clicking." Chicago Business, June 6, 2011. Retrieved July 2011 (http://www.chicagobusiness.com/article/20110604/ISSUE01/306049982/behind-dazzling-growth-story-groupon-struggles-to-keep-customers).

Podmolik, Mary Ellen. "Andrew Mason: CEO, Jester." *Chicago Tribune*, December 5, 2010. Retrieved July 2011 (http://articles.chicagotribune.com/2010-12-05/business/ct-biz-1205-groupon-mason-20101205_1_groupon-web-site-andrew-mason).

Raice, Shayndi. "Groupon Checks into Foursquare." *Wall Street Journal*, July 29, 2011. Retrieved August 2011 (http://blogs.wsj.com/digits/2011/07/29/groupon-checks-into-foursquare).

Rusli, Evelyn M. "What's Next for Groupon's Founder." *New York Times*, December 8, 2010. Retrieved July 2011 (http://dealbook.nytimes.com/2010/12/08/ whats-next-for-groupons-founder).

Saporito, Bill. "The Groupon Clipper." *TIME*, February 10, 2011. Retrieved August 2011 (http://www.time. com/time/magazine/article/0,9171,2048311,00.html).

Schroeder, Stan. "Groupon Buys Local Competitors, Expands to South Africa, India, and Israel." Mashable.com, January 11, 2011. Retrieved July 2011 (http://mashable.com/2011/01/11/groupon-south-africa-india-israel).

Sciullo, Maria. "Creativity and Confidence Propels Founder of Groupon, Mt. Lebanon Native Andrew Mason." *Pittsburgh Post-Gazette*, November 14, 2010. Retrieved July 2011 (http://www.post-gazette.com/ pg/10318/1103190-55.stm).

Sennett, Frank. "Groupon 2.0." *Time Out Chicago*, December 1, 2010. Retrieved July 2011 (http:// timeoutchicago.com/shopping-style/shopping/ 95595/groupon-20).

Steiner, Christopher. "Meet the Fastest-Growing Company Ever." *Forbes*, August 30, 2010. Retrieved August 2011 (http://www.forbes.com/forbes/2010/ 0830/entrepreneurs-groupon-facebook-twitter-next-web-phenom.html).

Streitfeld, David. "Funny or Die: Groupon's Fate Hinges on Words." *New York Times*, May 29, 2011. Retrieved August 2011 (http://www.nytimes.com/2011/05/29/business/29groupon.html?_r=1&sq=groupon&st=cse&scp=2&pagewanted=all).

Surowiecki, James. "Groupon Clipping." *New Yorker*, December 20, 2010. Retrieved August 2011 (http://www.newyorker.com/talk/financial/2010/12/20/ 101220ta_talk_surowiecki).

Swallow, Erica. "Groupon Smashes Sales Records with Nationwide Gap Deal." Mashable.com, August 19, 2010. Retrieved August 2011 (http://mashable.com/2010/08/19/gap-groupon).

Taulli, Tom. "Groupon Founders Spotty History a Cause for Concern." InvestorPlace, June 6, 2011. Retrieved July 2011 (http://www.investorplace.com/2011/06/groupon-grpn-andrew-mason-ceo-founder).

Taylor, Colleen. "Groupon's Updates IPO, by the Numbers." GigaOM, August 10, 2011. Retrieved September 2011 (http://gigaom.com/2011/08/10/groupon-ipo-update-filing).

Thia, Tyler. "Groupon China Downsizing Operations, Retrenching Employees." ZDNet Asia, August 25, 2011. Retrieved August 2011 (http://www.zdnetasia.com/groupon-china-downsizing-operations-retrenching-employees-62301801.htm).

Thomas, Owen. "Groupon Needs the Human Touch, Not Google's Robots." VentureBeat.com, November 19, 2010. Retrieved July 2011 (http://venturebeat.com/2010/11/19/groupon-google).

Thomas, Owen. "Rob Solomon: Too Rich for Groupon?" VentureBeat.com, March 23, 2011. Retrieved July 2011 ((http://venturebeat.com/2011/03/23/rob-solomon-groupon-secondary-markets).

Tuttle, Brad. "The Backlash Against Online Daily Deals." *TIME*, July 20, 2011. Retrieved August 2011 (http://moneyland.time.com/2011/07/20/daily-deal-backlash).

Tuttle, Brad. "How Humor Sells Silly Daily Deals No One Needs." Moneyland Blog/*TIME*, May 31, 2011. Retrieved July 2011 (http://moneyland.time.com/2011/05/31/how-humor-sells-silly-daily-deals-no-one-needs).

Tuttle, Brad. "Survey Stat I Don't Believe: About Half of Daily Deals Are for 'Needs,' and Half Are 'Wants.'" *TIME*, April 27, 2011. Retrieved August 2001 (http://moneyland.time.com/2011/04/27/survey-stat-i-dont-believe-about-half-of-daily-deals-are-for-needs-and-half-are-wants/#ixzz1WdzNF9Ph).

Van Grove, Jennifer. "Foursquare and Groupon Hook Up for Real-Time Deals." Mashable.com, July 29, 2011. Retrieved August 2011 (http://mashable.com/2011/07/29/foursquare-groupon-partnership).

Waldstein, Arnold. "What's Next for Groupon?" Social
Media Today, July 18, 2010. Retrieved July 2011
(http://socialmediatoday.com/arnoldwaldstein/
148464/what%E2%80%99s-next-groupon).

Wall Street Journal. "Groupon CEO's Non-Apology Letter
for Super Bowl Ad." February 7, 2011. Retrieved
July 2011 (http://blogs.wsj.com/venturecapital/
2011/02/07/groupon-ceos-non-apology-apology-
letter-for-super-bowl-ad).

Wauters, Robin. "Amazon Vet Jason Childs Joins Groupon
as CFO." TechCrunch.com, December 20, 2010.
Retrieved July 2011 (http://techcrunch.com/2010/12/
20/amazon-vet-jason-child-joins-groupon-as-cfo).

The Week. "IPO Jitters: Is Groupon 'Effectively
Insolvent'?" June 7, 2011. Retrieved July 2011 (http://
theweek.com/article/index/216044/ipo-jitters-is-
groupon-effectively-insolvent).

Weiss, Bari. "Groupon's $6 Billion Gambler." *Wall Street
Journal*, December 20, 2010. Retrieved July 2011
(http://online.wsj.com/article/SB10001424052748704
828104576021481410635432.html).

White, Charlie. "What's the Deal with Daily Deals?"
Mashable.com, September 10, 2011. Retrieved
September 2011 (http://mashable.com/2011/09/10/
daily-deals-infographic).

Williams, Geoff. "Groupon's Andrew Mason: The Unlikely
Dealmaker." AOL Small Business, August 9, 2010.

Retrieved August 2011 (http://smallbusiness.aol.com/2010/08/09/groupons-andrew-mason-the-unlikely-dealmaker).

Wong, Wailin. "Groupon's COO Leaves Company to Return to Google." *Chicago Tribune*, September 23, 2011. Retrieved September 2011 (http://www.chicagotribune.com/business/breaking/chi-groupons-coo-leaves-company-to-return-to-google-20110923,0,1164063.story).

Wortham, Jenna. "Start-Up Tries to Revive Online Group Buying." *New York Times*, September 15, 2009. Retrieved July 2011 (http://dealbook.nytimes.com/2009/09/18/start-up-tries-to-revive-online-group-buying).

Yadav, Sid. "Groupon Copies eBay's Playbook in International Buying Spree." VentureBeat.com, August 18, 2010. Retrieved August 2011 (http://www.venturebeat.com/2010/08/18/groupon-buying-spree-ebay-international).

Index

ABOUT THE AUTHOR

Philip Wolny is a writer and editor living in New York City. When he ventured forth online to find a bargain in this new era of the daily deal, he certainly found a plethora of choices that have recently dealt a blow to his natural thrift.

PHOTO CREDITS